*A General Introduction to the Great Books
and to a Liberal Education*

A
General Introduction
to the Great Books
and to a
Liberal Education

By
Mortimer J. Adler *and* Peter Wolff
with a Preface by
Robert M. Hutchins

ENCYCLOPÆDIA BRITANNICA, INC.

WILLIAM BENTON
Publisher

Chicago • London • Toronto • Geneva • Sydney • Tokyo • Manila

PREFACE

This first Reading Plan is called A General Introduction to the Great Books and to a Liberal Education.

What is a liberal education? It is easy to say what it is not. It is not specialized education, not vocational, avocational, professional or preprofessional. It is not an education that teaches a man how to do any specific thing.

I am tempted to say that it is the education that no American gets in an educational institution nowadays. We are all specialists now. Even early in high school we are told that we must begin to think how we are going to earn a living, and the prerequisites that are supposed to prepare us for that activity become more and more the ingredients of our educational diet. I am afraid we shall have to admit that the educational process in America is either a rather pleasant way of passing the time until we are ready to go to work, or a way of getting ready for some occupation, or a combination of the two. What is missing is education to be human beings, education to make the most of our human powers, education for our responsibilities as members of a democratic society, education for freedom.

This is what liberal education is. It is the education that prepares us to be free men. You have to have this education if you are going to be happy; for happiness consists in making the most of yourself. You have to have this education if you are going to be a member of the community; for membership in the community implies the ability to communicate with others. You have to have this education if you are going to be an effective citizen of a democracy; for citizenship requires that you understand the world in which you live and that you do not leave your duties to be performed by others, living vicariously and vacuously on their virtue and intelligence. A free society is a society composed of free men. To be free you have to be educated for freedom. This means that you have to think; for the free man is one who thinks for himself. It means that you have to think, for example, about the aims of life and of organized society. These are the questions raised by this first Reading Plan.

Perhaps I should say a little more about communication and community. Every specialist is trained in the jargon of his specialty. The tendency of specialization is that it grows narrower and narrower. The old definition of a specialist as a man who knows more and more about less and less is only too correct. As specialties grow narrower, the field of communication of each specialist narrows, too. He can talk about his specialty in the language of that specialty, but unless he can find another specialist in precisely the same specialty, he must either be tongue-tied or become a dreadful bore, discoursing on the subject he knows about but that the members of his audience do not understand, and doing so in a language incomprehensible to them.

And this is not all. On matters of common interest, like the activities of the community, the specialist is cut off from communication. More and more we hear the phrase: "That is outside my field," even though the subject is one that may mean life or death to the commonwealth, like education, automation, inflation, and nuclear energy. The Constitution of the United States does not require that all citizens shall be experts in everything. But its major premise, without which the whole democratic structure must collapse, is that the people will be informed enough, intelligent enough, and interested enough to judge the policies proposed to them by those whom they have chosen, with information, intelligence, and interest, to represent them.

The incentive to reading these books is not the acquisition of the formal proofs of education that Americans are accustomed to: credits, degrees, certificates, diplomas, etc. The incentive is simply your own desire to become as human as you can, for your own sake and that of your country. I have no doubt that you will become more "successful" in the usual definition of that term, because I cannot believe that it can be a handicap to a man to read and think and understand the tradition in which he lives. But whether or not you make more money and become more popular as a result of trying to acquire a liberal education, I can assure you that you will become a much more satisfactory companion to yourself.

Can you do it? Many people have. In the last twenty-five years hundreds of thousands of people have bought and read the Great Books, and discussed them with their family and friends and in organized groups of readers. Today at Aspen, Colorado, and in many business corporations numerous Americans have accepted seriously the obligation to understand the tradition of the Western world through these books.

Can you do it yourself? The purpose of this Reading Plan is to help you overcome the natural diffidence of any modest person in facing so impressive a collection as this set of books. You will see that the problems they deal with are current today. You will observe that the language is not nearly so difficult as you may have been told it is. The ideas are important; but they are not ideas that you have never heard of or have never thought about. These books were not written for specialists in philosophy or political science or literature; they were written for ordinary people, and read by them until it became fashionable to say, as it has lately, that they are too difficult for ordinary people.

These books are teachers. They demand attention, but if the attention is given, they reward it. As you read on, you will find the reading easier, for one book leads to another.

These books are, I believe, the finest written creations of the human mind. Our educational system largely disregards them. Even the names of some of the authors contained in this set are never mentioned in the presence of college students today. Yet these are the books that have made the world in which we live, and it is impossible to understand that world without understanding the principal positions taken in them.

A great adventure lies ahead of you as you take part in the Great Conversation.

Robert M. Hutchins

FOREWORD

It is the purpose of this Reading Plan to provide a way into the *Great Books* for readers who would like help in their first reading of them. Since this is a *general* introduction, no attempt has been made to orient this Reading Plan around one subject or one theme. Instead, we have tried to provide fifteen selections that are at once interesting, diverse, easy enough to be rewarding on a first reading, and difficult enough to offer a challenge to all readers—experts as well as beginners.

In fact, it might be said that the unifying theme of this series of reading is its diversity. We have tried to provide a fare that is varied enough to provide something for everyone. All of the following classifications are represented (of course, many works fall into more than one): poetry, prose, fiction, satire, tragedy, biography, autobiography, essay; politics, economics, ethics, philosophy, social science, history. The list could, of course, be extended.

Our reason for presenting such a variety is that it opens up three courses of study, any one of which you may follow.

1. If you decide that you like readings just like those on this list—i.e., if you would like to do more reading that is diverse in content and form—you will find additional reading lists of this sort in Volume I of the set. Starting on page 112 of that volume, there are ten reading lists (each one designed to make

ix

roughly one year of reading for a discussion group). These lists are very similar in makeup to the one in this Reading Plan; in fact, if you compare the First Year list with the one we have here you will find that over half of the readings are the same.

2. If you decide that some subject touched on in the Reading Plan before you interests you especially, you may want to do some extensive reading on that subject. For that reason we make other Reading Plans available to you which, unlike this one, are oriented around one subject or field of interest. Thus, if you should decide that you wish to read more in the field of politics, we have such a Reading Plan for you. Similarly, a Reading Plan is available should you decide that you would like to read more philosophy, etc.

3. If you decide that you want to read more about some topic that interests you—rather than cover a whole field like politics or philosophy—you may then go to the *Syntopicon*, and with the help of its Inventory of Terms and Outlines of Topics you will discover those special readings *within* the works that comprise the *Great Books* which bear on your interest.

You probably are already acquainted with Volume I (*The Great Conversation*) and with Volumes II and III (the *Syntopicon*), and know how to use them. But a few words may be in order to explain how to use this Reading Plan. It consists of three parts. There is (1) the reading list, (2) a guide to each of the readings, and (3) suggestions for additional readings.

1. The *number* of readings on the list—fifteen—was determined on the basis of approximately two weeks for each reading, which would make one normal academic year, from October through May. Similarly, the *length* of each reading is such that an adult can reasonably be expected to find time to finish it in a period of about two weeks. By far the longest selection (in number of pages) in this Reading Plan is Swift's *Gulliver's Travels;* it is almost twice the length of the next most extended, Plutarch's *Lives.* Both of these are, of course, much easier to read, because of their narrative form, than works that require detailed attention to their analysis and

exposition (as, for example, the shortest reading on the list, Book I of Aristotle's *Nicomachean Ethics*).

2. We hope that the second part of this plan, containing fifteen guides to the readings, will be of most help to the reader who is making his way through the *Great Books* without any other teachers, discussion group leader or printed aid.

The guides try to help you to get started on a particular assignment, to provide some necessary background and information, and to stimulate your thinking about the book under consideration.

To do all this, various devices are used. Biographical material concerning the author is provided, especially where it is relevant to his writings. Often you will also find some information concerning the historical circumstances under which the book was written, or concerning the historical period that it describes. The latter is done particularly for writing that is itself historical.

Frequently, the guide will include a consideration of the art form of the book being studied. For example, there are discussions of the dialogue as a style of exposition, and the question is raised as to its suitability for philosophical writing. Again, the difference between historical and poetic writing is discussed.

A large portion of each guide is devoted to the content of the assignment. The highlights of the reading are pointed out, sometimes by quotation. Passages that are known to present difficulties are discussed and explained. The structure of the whole book is considered and the individual parts are related to it. Above all, an attempt is made to indicate the relevance of the book and what it says to present-day situations and issues.

Special attention is given to problems for you, the critical reader, to think about. These are not posed as mere questions, however. Each statement of a problem is followed by one or more paragraphs illuminating it, indicating some of the possible answers, and noting the importance of the question. Some readers will be satisfied simply to read these problems, and to give them some thought; others may want actually to write out answers to them. An answer will not consist of a mere "yes" or "no," or "true" or "false." Each problem requires real analysis and an answer may take one or two paragraphs or even a full essay. Since there is no "right" answer to these questions, and since their main purpose is to stimulate some thought about the reading matter, you alone will be able to check and judge your answer.

Each guide concludes with a section entitled Self-Testing Questions. This section gives you an opportunity to check the thoroughness of your reading and contains a series of questions—anywhere from half a dozen to a dozen—about the reading. They are factual questions and can therefore be answered in a definite fashion. The information needed to give the answer will be found on some page of the reading assignment. The right answer can, therefore, be simply indicated by reference to a page or pages from the reading assignment. In order to give you an opportunity to check yourself, these references are given on pages 189-191.

3. The Additional Readings section is almost self-explanatory. It provides you with an opportunity to go deeper into the subject that particularly interests you. Because so many subjects are touched upon, we have keyed the additional readings to the original fifteen readings. Furthermore, in this Reading Plan, we have restricted ourselves to suggesting additional readings from Great Books that touch on the same subject. In other Reading Plans, we have recommended additional readings from works not included in Great Books.

CONTENTS

A NOTE ON
REFERENCE STYLE

In referring to *Great Books* the same style is used as in the *Syntopicon*. Pages are cited by number and section. In books that are printed in single column, "a" and "b" refer to the upper and lower half of the page. In books that are printed in double column, "a" and "b" refer to the upper and lower half of the left column, "c" and "d" to the upper and lower half of the right column. For example, "Vol. 53, p. 210b" refers to the lower half of page 210, since Vol. 53, James's *Principles of Psychology,* is printed in single column. But "Vol. 7, p. 202b" refers to the lower left quarter of page 202, since Vol. 7, Plato's *Dialogues,* is printed in double column.

In Bible references, if there is a difference between the King James and the Douay version, the King James reference is given first, followed by (D) and the Douay reference.

THE READING LIST

PLATO

Apology and *Crito*

Vol. 7, pp. 200–219

P lato's report of the trial of Socrates and of his last days in prison vividly dramatizes for us one of the most moving events in the history of the human race. The charges brought against Socrates by the Athenians of his day typify the accusations which, in other countries and at other times, have been leveled against men who have been single-minded in their adherence to ideals that have set them apart from the society in which they lived.

Society usually recognizes its debt to such men after it has martyred them. But such men have seldom recognized, as clearly as Socrates did, the reason for society's driving passion to silence them. The turning point in his trial—the moment of truth—occurs when Socrates confesses to being a gadfly and so admits that he has been and will continue to be a disturber of the peace, the peace of mind of those who do not wish to think, not just the Athenians of the 5th century B.C., but all men everywhere.

I

If, as Alfred North Whitehead wrote (in *Process and Reality*), "the European philosophical tradition consists of a series of footnotes to Plato," then there can be no better starting place than Plato for an introduction to the *Great Books*. Indeed, there is probably no other philosopher who is so universally honored as Plato. Other philosophers have, at certain times, been more influential than Plato, as Aristotle in the middle ages, and perhaps Kant and Hegel in the nineteenth century. And many philosophers, from Plato's foremost pupil Aristotle onwards, have vigorously disagreed with him on many points. Nevertheless, with very few exceptions, all philosophers acknowledge their debt to Plato and are moved, in their remarks about him and his teacher, Socrates, by what can only be described as a kind of piety.

The source of this remarkable affection and honor that is bestowed on Plato is nowhere clearer than in these two dialogues. It derives in large part from the figure of Socrates, who is here presented as a man of truly remarkable uprightness and courage. Plato is bound to be at least in part identified with Socrates, for most of what we know about Socrates, and everything that we know about his philosophical views, comes to us from Plato.

Nevertheless, we must distinguish between Socrates and Plato as historical persons. They are not the same man; but one of them, Plato, always puts what he has to say into the mouths of others—mostly that of Socrates.

In the dialogues, therefore, it is always Plato who is speaking, although his skill as a writer of dialogue is such that we can easily forget that this is so and imagine that it is Socrates who is addressing us. In order to help produce this illusion, Plato is not above using such tricks as mentioning himself by name. In the *Apology* his name occurs twice: once on page 208b, where Socrates mentions "Adeimantus the son of Ariston, whose brother Plato is present" and again on page 210b, where Plato is mentioned as one of Socrates' friends who bid him propose a fine of thirty minae as his punishment, for which they will be security. Still, there is no attempt at deception here; Plato's works have always been known as Plato's, not Socrates'.

It would also be wrong to assume that in writing the dialogues, Plato acted as a mere recorder of conversation between Socrates and his interlocutors. Plato put into the mouths of the participants what he thought they might have said and what he thought Socrates would have said. Thus we certainly do not have verbatim reports here; Socrates' adversaries are probably more obstreperous than they were in real life and Socrates is probably more patient and more wise than he was in real life. Nevertheless, though the content of the dialogues is Plato's, and though the manner of the dialogue may have been altered by him, the general impression which Plato wanted to create was certainly that this was the sort of dialogue that Socrates was involved in, and these were the sorts of things that he discussed, and these were the kinds of conclusions to which he came.

Furthermore, many of the participants in the dialogues as written by Plato are known to have been actual contemporaries of Socrates. Not all were mere youths, but many were older and well-known persons. Thus Gorgias and Protagoras, who figure prominently in the dialogues named after them, were famous Sophists; Alcibiades, who makes his appearance in the *Symposium*, was sufficiently famous and infamous to be a subject of Plutarch's *Lives;* and one of the participants in the *Laches* is the general Nicias, who is mentioned often in Thucydides' *History of the Peloponnesian War* (see Vol. 6). We may assume, therefore, that not only the names were

patterned after real persons, but that also what they said was
patterned after what took place between them and Socrates.

Socrates' trial and execution took place in the year 399 B.C.
Socrates was then seventy years of age, and Plato, twenty-nine.
(He may not have written the account of these events until a
few years later, however.) The three accusers of Socrates were
Meletus, Anytus, and Lycon. (See p. 203b.)

Why did Athens put her most famous citizen to death? The
charges and Socrates' answers to them are discussed in the
Apology, where we can examine them. However, it may help
to understand the trial (though not to justify its outcome) if
we remember the political situation at Athens at the time. In
404 B.C. Athens concluded, in defeat, twenty-seven years of almost continuous warfare with Sparta and her allies. This bitter
period of Athenian history is recorded for us in Thucydides'
History of the Peloponnesian War; it was followed by severe
political upheavals. Democracy, which had been the form of
government in Athens for a hundred years, was replaced by an
oligarchy, the government of the Thirty (Socrates alludes to it
on p. 207 c–d). But the oligarchy did not last and was replaced
again by democracy, more anti-oligarchical in character than
ever. It was this democratic government which tried Socrates.
Socrates, we may add, was suspected of being in favor of the
oligarchical government. The passage on page 207, however,
shows him unwilling to commit injustice, whether ordered to
do so by democrats or by oligarchs.

II

In the course of his defense, Socrates paints a picture of himself. We may, therefore, be sure that Socrates' portrait is as
favorable to him as truth and the exigencies of a court trial
would permit. And it is probably no exaggeration to say that
hardly anyone can read the account without feeling that a
grave injustice was done. No doubt that feeling is also accom-
panied by considerable amazement that the Athenians could
so misunderstand Socrates as to find him guilty. No matter
how much weight we give to political considerations which

might predispose the court against Socrates, the fact remains that a grave judicial miscarriage is unfolded before our eyes.

Just because of this nearly unanimous feeling of outrage at what the Athenians have perpetrated, we may do well to examine how we ourselves would react to Socrates, or to a man very much like Socrates, if he were brought to trial in our times.

He is certainly uncompromising: "Men of Athens," he says,

> I honour and love you; but I shall obey God rather than you, and while I have life and strength I shall never cease from the practice and teaching of philosophy. . . . (p. 206b)

These remarks are made in Socrates' first, long speech, which constitutes his main defense. Even after he has already been condemned, however, and is required to suggest a penalty for himself, Socrates voices the same sentiments:

> If I tell you . . . that I cannot hold my tongue, you will not believe that I am serious; and if I say again that daily to discourse about virtue, and of those other things about which you hear me examining myself and others, is the greatest good of man, and that the unexamined life is not worth living, you are still less likely to believe me. Yet I say what is true, although a thing of which it is hard for me to persuade you. (p. 210b)

Far from being penitent and humble, he asserts—with what must have sounded to his judges like consummate arrogance—his intention to continue his offensive ways; and even after he has been found guilty he persists in saying that he will not change. No doubt his second refusal to change made a fatal impression on his judges. We may imagine, without considering the rightness of the doctrines involved, the effect such intransigence would have on a court or investigating committee in a "cold war" situation where a Communist in a Capitalist country not only refused to recant but announced his determination to continue his "subversive" activities; or, of course, the effect of such a position taken by a Capitalist in a Communist country.

But let us return to Socrates' defense of himself; the state needs him, he maintains:

I am not going to argue for my own sake, as you may think, but for yours, that you may not sin against the God by condemning me, who am his gift to you. For if you kill me you will not easily find a successor to me, who, if I may use such a ludicrous figure of speech, am a sort of gadfly, given to the state by God; and the state is a great and noble steed who is tardy in his motions owing to his very size, and requires to be stirred into life. I am that gadfly which God has attached to the state, and all day long and in all places am always fastening upon you, arousing and persuading and reproaching you. (p. 207a)

No matter how accurate this description of Socrates may be—and we may assume that it is perfectly true—it cannot have helped but arouse the animosity of his listeners. We can only hope that in a similar situation nowadays, the case would be judged on its merits, even if the defendant proved as imprudent as we here find Socrates. It may of course have been known to Socrates, as well as to Plato, that in any case Socrates' cause was lost, and that, therefore, the best he could hope for would be a public opportunity to say how *he* looked upon himself and what *he* felt were the true causes of the accusation and its outcome.

The *Crito* not only carries Socrates' biography forward, it also gives us a good example of the Socratic method. It is of special interest here to see Socrates conversing on an abstract moral problem derived from his own case, since it enables us to judge the charges that were brought against him.

The problem under discussion is a man's, especially a citizen's, relation to the laws of his state. To Crito, the situation seems, at least initially, very simple. Socrates has been unjustly condemned to die, having been convicted of corrupting the youth—a crime which Crito certainly knows Socrates is not guilty of, since Crito's own son, Critobulus, was under Socrates' influence (as we learn in the *Apology*). Hence, Crito concludes, friendship demands and justice condones his assistance in Socrates' escape. But Socrates, following his own counsel that "the unexamined life is not worth living," proceeds to question Crito's position, and, ultimately, to reject it.

III

We may now examine both the *Apology* and the *Crito* and ask some questions about them.

Should an unjust law be obeyed?

Here by an "unjust law" is meant a law that is unjust in content, i.e., that commands some unjust action or prohibits some just action. Contemporary examples of this might be racially discriminatory statutes. Many good citizens—even non-drinkers—held the Volstead Act to be an invasion of human rights. Some pacifists oppose taxation for military purposes, and some religious groups oppose vaccination, compulsory education, or the pledge to the flag. What is a conscientious citizen to do about laws he really believes to be unjust? Should he disobey them? Or are there reasons for obeying even an unjust law?

What can be done when a law is unjustly applied?

A law may be just and good, but it may still have been un-justly applied. A famous example of this sort of thing was the Dreyfus case in France. The law involved—calling for the punishment of traitors—would seem to be just. It was unjustly applied, however, since Captain Dreyfus was not guilty of treason. Here again, the citizen must ask himself what his duty is. How, first of all, can he be certain that a law has been justly or unjustly applied? Most of us tend to rely on the assumption that the judicial system is infallible; i.e., when someone has been duly tried and been found guilty by a jury, we assume that justice has been done. But juries and judges are men and men are fallible. We know that there are miscarriages of justice; innocent men are convicted, probably every day. Many eminent Americans think that Sacco and Vanzetti, executed in 1927 for the murder of a payroll clerk, were innocent; and after years in prison for throwing a bomb during the San Francisco Preparedness Day Parade of 1916,

Tom Mooney was pardoned by a governor who was convinced that Mooney was unjustly convicted.

But there is also a second problem. Suppose that there is no doubt whatever about the unjust application of the law, no doubt that the wrong man has been accused, what are we to do then? Does the duty of the citizen demand obedience or disobedience?

What are a citizen's duties and responsibilities when a law is not duly made?

A law may be just in content, but may have been unjustly made. This would happen if a good law was not made by due legislative process, but say, was imposed as a decree. If, in other words, it is the job of the legislature to make laws, then any administrative decree—no matter how good in content and intent—does not have the force of law, since it was not made by the legislature.

Was Socrates justified in disobeying an explicit command, because it was unjust (see p. 207d)?

In the *Crito*, Socrates refuses to disobey the laws; yet in the case which he reports in the *Apology*, he had no hesitation to disobey an order. How were the two situations different, if at all? Can his apparently contradictory positions be reconciled? Can we reconcile his support of law in the *Crito* with his asserted intention, in the *Apology*, to obey God rather than his judges?

In what sense was Socrates a wise man?

The answer that comes immediately to mind, of course, is that he had the wisdom of knowing that he did not know. What needs to be investigated, however, is whether this is truly wisdom, or whether this is only a play on words. Is the mere knowledge of one's own ignorance the highest achievement of the intellect? To indicate that there are some hidden difficulties here, let us consider the skeptic, who will not accept anything as certainly true. He, too, may characterize him-self as knowing that he does not know. Does this mean that Socrates is a skeptic? Or that Socrates' and the skeptic's wis-dom is the same?

Furthermore, are there not a good many things that Socra-tes seems to know? In the *Crito*, he certainly acts like someone who knows something about law, duty, and citizenship. What then is the meaning of his ignorance and his wisdom?

How do you interpret the statement "The un-examined life is not worth living"?

What about one's life should be examined? And is this an injunction that applies to everyone or only to Socrates? Or does it apply only to philosophers, but not to businessmen, lawyers, laborers, artists, etc.? How can the demands of daily living be reconciled with the demand for self-examination? How does one go about examining one's life? And is the intro-spective person, who examines and re-examines everything he does, necessarily living a worthwhile life?

The following questions are designed to help you test the thoroughness of your reading. Each question is to be answered by giving a page or pages of the reading assignment. Answers will be found on page 189 of this Reading Plan.

1 What are the old charges against Socrates?

2 What are the new charges?

3 In his search for a wise man, Socrates came upon a group of people who did know something. Who were they?

4 How does Socrates defend himself against the charge of being an atheist?

5 Why can no one injure Socrates? Why is death better than life?

6 Why do the laws feel that Socrates' escape would injure them?

PLATO

The Republic

Books I–II

Vol. 7, pp. 295–324

Who among us has not, at some time in his life, complained of being unjustly treated? Are there any parents who have not heard such complaints from children, or who have never paused to consider whether some reward or punishment to be meted out is just? Every human being in one capacity or another—as employer or employee, as buyer or seller, as officer or soldier, as plaintiff or defendant, as governor or governed—has probably demanded justice or faced the demand for it. But though all of us have asked *for* justice, few of us have asked *about* it; and even if we have, we probably felt, like Pilate, that there was no point in waiting for an answer.

That is the question Plato asks in *The Republic* and asks in a way that persuades us to pursue the answer—patiently and at length. It is not an easy question, but Plato makes us feel that it is an inescapable one if we are at all concerned to understand our innate sense of right and wrong. In the opening books of *The Republic*, he challenges each of us to examine his conscience on that very point. How strong is our sense of right and wrong? Would it restrain us from doing wrong to others if we could profit by it and get away with it? Do we really think that might is not right, or only when we feel that the right is on our side and know that the might is on the other fellow's?

Second Reading

I

The ten books of *The Republic* (the Greek word might also be translated by "polity" or simply by "state") constitute the second longest of Plato's dialogues, being exceeded in length only by the twelve books of the *Laws*. It is therefore necessary to read this dialogue in several parts, and we naturally begin with the first two books. Unfortunately, the division into books does not always agree with the division that the organization of the work would seem to demand. Thus, in the present case, a definite unit of discussion seems to end with Book I; but the next division does not seem to come at the end of Book II, but rather a little earlier, namely on page 316b. For it is there that the question "What is justice?" is temporarily put aside, and a new question "What is the state?" is begun to be investigated. If you find the length of this reading burdensome, therefore, page 316b is a good place to stop short. (The second book of the dialogue is assigned again in the Reading Plan on *Politics*.)

These remarks also indicate that there is necessarily something unsatisfactory about reading merely a portion rather than the whole of a work. Some questions are bound to be left unanswered until the whole book has been read. But this does not mean that *all* questions are unanswered, or that no profit can be gained from a partial reading. The dialogue form that Plato employs for his writings gives us an important hint as to how we can defend reading less than the whole.

Unlike straight expository writing, which—at least when it is well done—indicates clearly at the beginning what problem is being examined and then proceeds to analyze and, if possible, solve that problem, the dialogue, even when it is complete and even when it is written by a master like Plato, does not proceed in such straightforward fashion. It is often not the first question that comes up which is the main topic of a dialogue; and because of the question-and-answer form it is sometimes not easy to decide which is Plato's opinion. Furthermore, more often than not a dialogue does not end with a clearly formulated conclusion, but rather with a problem that still remains to be solved.

In all this, of course, the dialogue merely imitates actual spoken discourse. Anyone who has ever participated in a discussion knows that it often takes considerable time before an important question even becomes formulated, and that the discussion often breaks up before the question is answered to everyone's satisfaction. Further, it is a commonplace that an answer may raise more problems than it solves. Nevertheless, it is easily possible to distinguish between a good and a bad oral discussion. The same criteria will also apply to the distinction between a good and a bad dialogue in writing.

A good discussion or a good dialogue must at least achieve this much: the problem or problems which it attacks must come to be sharply defined; the terms employed in stating the questions and answers must be clarified; it should indicate how an answer to the problem would commit the answerer to positions on other questions. A good discussion, in other words, causes its participants to learn something.

These same criteria can obviously be applied also to portions of a dialogue. Just as it is possible to learn something from participating in part of a discussion—though not as much as from the whole—so it is possible to profit from reading part of a dialogue, provided only that it results in some clarification and re-thinking of problems. In the light of these criteria, the first two books of *The Republic* certainly constitute a very good unit of reading; at the same time, it is to be hoped that reading them will also leave you with a desire to read the rest of the work.

II

Since these two books of *The Republic* cover a good many pages, it may be helpful if you hold before yourself the several parts into which they are divided.

Book I

A. There is (as in many, though not all dialogues) an introductory section (295a–296a). It gives the setting and introduces the persons of the dialogue.

B. This is followed by Socrates' discourse with the old man, Cephalus (296a-297c). It ends precisely at the point where the question is reached, "What is justice?"

C. The argument is inherited by Cephalus' son, Polemarchus, who tries unsuccessfully to defend the definition of justice as "doing good to your friends and harm to your enemies" (297a–300b).

D. Here Thrasymachus jumps into the argument and tries to maintain that "justice is the interest of the stronger." Socrates shows that this is not so. At the end of this section, however, which is also the end of Book I, Socrates says that though he has said many things about what justice is not, and what its attributes are, he has not yet found out what justice is (300b–310c).

Book II

E. Glaucon revives the argument. The majority of mankind, he says, hold injustice to be superior to justice. He tells the story of the wonderful ring of Gyges (310c–313a).

F. Adeimantus, Glaucon's brother, adds that *appearing* just rather than *being* just is advantageous. He asks Socrates to refute him and his brother by discussing the nature of justice (313a–316a).

G. Socrates agrees, but wants to look for justice in the state rather than in man, since it will more easily be seen in the larger unit. He begins by envisaging how a very simple and plain state would come into being (316a–318b).

H. Socrates goes on to treat of the luxurious state, which almost at once becomes involved in war and so needs warriors or guardians (318b–320c).

I. Socrates turns to the education of these guardians. They must be told the truth, not poetic lies, about the nature of the gods. This ends Book II (320c–324c).

III

Let us put some flesh on this skeletal outline by indicating what some of the highlights of the discussion are. The persistent theme, of course, is justice, and so we shall begin by tracing the various definitions of justice that are offered, and seeing why they are rejected.

The first definition is offered, almost casually, by Cephalus, in response to Socrates' question concerning the advantages of wealth:

> The great blessing of riches, I do not say to every man, but to a good man, is, that he has had no occasion to deceive or to defraud others, either intentionally or unintentionally. . . . (297b)

Socrates at once goes beyond Cephalus' words:

> Well said, Cephalus, I replied; but as concerning justice, what is it?—to speak the truth and to pay your debts—no more than this? (297b–c)

Socrates challenges the adequacy of this, because there are obviously some cases where one ought not to pay one's debts. But Cephalus refuses to be drawn into an argument and Polemarchus undertakes to defend his view by referring to the poet Simonides, who "said that the repayment of a debt is just." Socrates modifies this a little:

> Simonides . . . after the manner of poets, would seem to have spoken darkly of the nature of justice; for he really meant to say that justice is the giving to each man what is proper to him, and this he termed a debt. (298a)

Now, of course, the question arises "what is due to each man?" The answer is not long in forthcoming:

If, Socrates, we are to be guided at all by the analogy of the preceding instances, then justice is the art which gives good to friends and evil to enemies. (298a)

This too, however, turns out to be unsatisfactory. It can be maintained, Socrates shows, that it is never just to injure anyone, whether friend or enemy.

Then if a man says that justice consists in the repayment of debts, and that good is the debt which a man owes to his friends, and evil the debt which he owes to his enemies—to say this is not wise; for it is not true, if, as has been clearly shown, the injuring of another can be in no case just. (300a)

Although this finishes Polemarchus, we should notice that Socrates' refutation succeeds only because Polemarchus has identified what is due to each man as *good* in the case of friends, and *evil* in the case of enemies. If he had defined a man's due in some other fashion, Socrates' line of argument would have had to be different, and it is at least *possible* that the definition of justice as "each man's due" might have been successfully defended. What gets Polemarchus into trouble, of course, is that he associated justice, which is a virtue, with doing evil.

But Socrates does not lack opponents, for now Thrasymachus springs into the battle. He is more remarkable for his pugnaciousness than for his ability in argument; although in fairness to Thrasymachus we should point out that he makes another appearance in the dialogue in Book V, where he is most docile and friendly to Socrates. Here in Book I, however, he is aggressive and overbearing; Socrates, however, soon "gives him his due," a thorough refutation.

"Justice is nothing else than the interest of the stronger" is what Thrasymachus proclaims (301b–c). This statement is a little puzzling, until it becomes clear that what Thrasymachus means to say is this: whatever the stronger man does is just; and the stronger man always acts for his *own* interest. In a state, as between ruler and ruled, the stronger is of course the ruler. But Socrates won't let this pass:

> There is no one in any rule who, in so far as he is a ruler, con-
> siders or enjoins what is for his own interest, but always what is
> for the interest of his subject or suitable to his art; to that he looks,
> and that alone he considers in everything which he says and does.
> (303d–304a)

Thrasymachus counters that Socrates' view of ruler and ruled
is outrageous; the ruler rules for his own interest not that of
the ruled, just as the shepherd rules the sheep for his own interest (to provide himself with food and wool) not for the interest of the sheep.

Socrates quickly turns the shepherd-sheep argument
against Thrasymachus. When a shepherd rules the sheep for
the sake of providing a meal for himself, he is then not acting
as a shepherd but as an eater; when he rules the sheep for the
sake of making money, he is not acting as a shepherd but as a
money-maker.

> You thought that the shepherd as a shepherd tends the sheep not with
> a view to their own good, but like a mere diner or banquetter with a
> view to the pleasures of the table; or, again, as a trader for sale in the
> market, and not as a shepherd. Yet surely the art of the shepherd
> is concerned only with the good of his subjects; he has only to
> provide the best for them, since the perfection of the art is already
> ensured whenever all the requirements of it are satisfied. And that
> was what I was saying just now about the ruler. I conceived that the
> art of the ruler, considered as ruler, whether in a state or in pri-
> vate life, could only regard the good of his flock or subjects.
> (305a–b)

This is not all that goes on in Book I, but enough to give
the main outlines. Here we can now see a surprising development. Socrates' refutation of Thrasymachus gives us, by impli-
cation, the definition of a ruler's justice as "acting for the sake
of the ruled," or "acting so as to give the ruled their due."
Now this is entirely compatible with Polemarchus' earlier definition of justice as "acting so as to give each man his due."
That latter definition only failed to satisfy Socrates because
Polemarchus was mistaken about what each man's due is. If
Socrates' definition of justice is valid, he must show what it is

that is due to those who are ruled. And, of course, a great part of *The Republic* is devoted to just that.

IV

Book II makes an entirely fresh start; all the participants of the earlier book are, as it were, forgotten, with the exception of Socrates. The question concerning the nature of justice is now raised, first by Glaucon and then by his brother Adeimantus. It will afford a moment's amusement if we disregard the content of the dialogue temporarily, and consider the personalities involved.

Glaucon and Adeimantus are pictured far more favorably than any one else we have met in the dialogue so far. Cephalus is very old, but his wisdom does not seem to have kept step with his age; he abandoned the search for justice at the crucial moment "and went away laughing." Polemarchus hardly seems very bright; and Thrasymachus is vainglorious and rude. Glaucon and Adeimantus, on the other hand, are very bright, docile but not fawning, and genuinely interested in the argument.

Who are these two? We know from a remark made in the Apology (208b) that Adeimantus (and hence also Glaucon) are Plato's brothers. Thus, there is a double meaning in Socrates' exhortation to Adeimantus "Let brother help brother" (ostensibly referring only to Glaucon by this remark), and again when Socrates praises Glaucon and Adeimantus as "divine offspring of an illustrious father."

We turn now to the contribution which the brothers make to the search for justice. In the main, they present a much more refined picture of the unjust man than was presented in Book I. This refinement is suggested by the story of the ring of Gyges.

If a man can *appear* just while really being unjust, they argue, then he will have the best possible life. Simply to be unjust, without being careful to appear just, as Thrasymachus held, is too crude, for then a man is subject to the censure of public opinion, as well as to legal punishment.

There seem to be two ways of avoiding punishment: either by appearing just, or by being just (though in this latter case the appearance is also important, since the man who is just but appears to be unjust is likely to be punished). Since a man can act much more advantageously for himself by being unjust (i.e., by taking advantage of other people) than by being just, there never is any reason to be just, unless that happens to be the only way to present the appearance of justice.

Though the last statement may seem outrageous, it in fact expresses a common sentiment. What do people mean when they say "Honesty is the best policy"? Whether consciously or not, they do not recommend honesty for its own sake, or because it is just, but rather as a *policy*, i.e., as an expedient way of acting for a purpose. *Policies* are changed if they do not achieve their purpose. Hence it would seem that, if honesty does not achieve its purpose (the appearance of justice and the gain of one's selfish aim), then some policy other than honesty should be followed.

Adeimantus gives this testimony to show that what mankind really desires is the appearance of justice only:

> For what men say is that, if I am really just and am not also thought just, profit there is none, but the pain and loss on the other hand are unmistakeable. But if, though unjust, I acquire the reputation of justice, a heavenly life is promised to me. Since then, as philosophers prove, appearance tyrannizes over truth and is lord of happiness, to appearance I must devote myself. I will describe around me a picture and shadow of virtue to be the vestibule and exterior of my house; behind I will trail the subtle and crafty fox. . . . (314b–c)

Glaucon and Adeimantus exhibit the advantages of injustice so energetically in order to hear Socrates refute these views and have him praise justice as a great good. And that is what he proceeds to do, by looking once more for the nature of justice, and beginning with justice in the state rather than in the individual.

V

Now let us raise some problems about this dialogue. The first few have to do with the method that Socrates (or Plato) employs; then we shall turn to questions of content.

Can the question "What is justice?" be settled by looking the word "justice" up in a dictionary?

Perhaps the best way to answer this question is to try the dictionary method. We find the following in *Webster's Unabridged Dictionary* under "justice": "The maintenance or administration of that which is just; just treatment. . . ." It goes on like that. Since "justice" is here defined in terms of "just" we may imagine that we might have better luck with that word. Here are the initial entries under "just": "1. Conforming to the spiritual law; righteous; specif., righteous before God. 2. Righteous, or conforming to what is righteous, in the dealing of one man with another; equitable in action or judgment; impartial; . . ."

Suppose we have one more try and look up "righteous": "Doing, or according with, that which is right; just; upright; equitable; . . ."

No more need be said to show that this circular process does not get at what Socrates wants when he asks "What is justice?"

Is Socrates on the right track when he looks for a definition of justice? Would his purpose be better served by giving him examples of just men and just actions?

To look for a definition of justice is to assume that there is some one thing called "justice" waiting to be defined. But perhaps that assumption is unjustified. And even if there is one thing called "justice," how do we know that it could not be better made known to us by examples than by definitions?

This question is of considerable importance. It would seem that both general definitions and particular examples have their role in philosophical discussion. What needs to be assessed is how they are to be used together. As we read further in the Platonic dialogues, this relationship will become clearer.

Is Socrates justified in looking for justice in the state rather than in man? May not a just state and a just person have different kinds of justice?

This question is related to the previous one, of course. Socrates seems to take for granted that a man and a state are sufficiently alike to possess the same justice. Yet could one not argue that "large" means something different when applied to a man and when applied to a state, and that therefore "just" may also mean something different in the two cases?

What is the end or purpose of any art?

Socrates is famous for his examples taken from arts, usually very common and simple arts; hence it is important to become clear about the notion of an art. In the first book of *The Republic*, the art of the shepherd is used in a crucial fashion.

Most of the arts mentioned in *The Republic* involve an artist and a living subject of the art, such as sheep, or sailors, or patients. It is to the interest of these subjects that an art is said to look. But what would Socrates do about other kinds of art; for example, the arts of cooking, reading, singing? Or the fine arts, which we usually first think of when the word "art" is used, that is, the arts of painting, poetry, sculpture, etc.?

What is the origin of war, according to Socrates?

Do you agree that war necessarily arises from luxury? This question is interesting when you consider the related question of whether war is inevitable. If war is only due to luxury, it would seem that the elimination of the one would lead to the elimination of the other. Apparently, however, what Plato calls luxuries are so difficult to eliminate that he does not even consider the possibility. In fact, he passes very quickly from the plain to the luxurious state and never comes back to the former. Does such a "plain" state exist, or has one ever existed in the past? What is the "luxurious" state, and how does it get that way? What is the relationship of luxury and civilization, of luxury and peace?

As we shall see when we have read more of *The Republic*, Plato introduces a warrior class into his state, not only easily but with pleasure Apparently, though *The Republic* is often called a utopia, perpetual peace was not one of Plato's utopian ideals.

Why does Socrates favor censorship in his state?

Modern thinking is so accustomed to regard censorship as an evil, that it is surprising that Plato never even considers the possibility that there might be some arguments against it. Of course, arguments against censorship based on the desirability of a democratic form of government will cut no ice with Plato. It would be interesting, therefore, to try to find some reasons against censorship that are not based on a particular form of government. And we should consider censorship (both governmental and non-governmental) in our own society, censorship of speech, assembly, association, and action, as well as of the arts (e.g., books, movies, plays, etc.).

The following questions are designed to help you test the thoroughness of your reading. Each question is to be answered by giving a page or pages of the reading assignment. Answers will be found on page 189 of this Reading Plan.

1 What does Cephalus think are the advantages of old age?

2 What does Socrates say are the three questions that he has considered in Book I?

3 What is the story of the ring of Gyges?

4 What is the origin of the state?

5 Why does a state need a *separate* warrior class?

6 What are the two main divisions of education according to Socrates?

7 Why is there to be censorship of the poets?

SOPHOCLES

Oedipus the King and *Antigone*

Vol. 5, pp. 99–113, 131–142

Like the word "happy," the word "tragic" is one that men use in a wide variety of senses. Yet all of us share the sense that these adjectives are as opposite in their meaning as "white" and "black." In this we are probably carrying over from our school days the memory that a tragic play, such as *Hamlet* or *Romeo and Juliet,* is one that does not have a happy ending. But what is true of dramas—that they cannot be both happy and tragic—may not be true of human lives. On the contrary, the deepest trait of our earthly existence may be that the element of tragedy enters into the lives of all of us, even the happiest of mortals.

These two tragedies of Sophocles help us to understand this. Though one is the story of a king and the other the story of a princess, what befalls them could befall any of us. Oedipus and Antigone are each confronted with a choice between alternatives, neither of which can possibly turn out well. Yet they must choose. There is no escaping that. Nor, having chosen, can they escape the consequences of their choice. Were they not free to choose, the catastrophe that overtakes them would not be of their own making, but purely the work of fate.

All of us, in small measure or great, have tasted the bitterness of defeat at our own hands, unavoidable because we must choose and cannot find an alternative that is not fraught with evil. This is the tragic element which, once we see it writ large in the tragedies of Oedipus and Antigone, we can detect in our own lives and in those of all around us.

Third Reading

I

Sophocles was born about 495 B.C. and died in 406 B.C. He is thus an older contemporary of Socrates (469–399 B.C.), and was already sixty-seven years old when Plato was born (in 428 B.C.). Plato mentions him by name in the first book of *The Republic*, where he has the old man, Cephalus, refer to "the aged poet Sophocles." Sophocles' life coincides with the rise and fall of Athens; he was born just before the victory over the Persians at Marathon (490 B.C.) and he died just before the end of the disastrous Peloponnesian War (404 B.C.) which forever terminated Athens' hopes of being a great military power. He lived through the golden age of Athens; indeed we may fairly say that Sophocles was one of those men whose achievements gave that age its luster. So undisputed was Athens' leadership in the arts and sciences that Pericles in a famous speech boasted, "as a city we are the school of Hellas." (See Vol. 6, p. 397c)

Sophocles is said to have written 120 plays; only seven of them survive. He competed for the tragic prize in the annual competition thirty-two times; he won at least eighteen times. We may certainly assume that *Oedipus the King* represents one such victory. It has always been considered a model of tragedy; Aristotle in *On Poetics* draws on it more than on any other play to illustrate his points. We shall mention a few of the things that Aristotle says about tragedy and *Oedipus the King* after first spending a little time on the play itself.

II

Oedipus the King is the longest of the extant Sophoclean tragedies, although it is not half as long as *Hamlet* or *Othello*.

Oedipus the King gives the impression of tremendous compactness. It is constructed with such economy that there seems to be no superfluous word in it; every utterance of the actors contributes to the rush toward its climax. The play is so unified and well-knit that it is often difficult to keep the various parts of the plot separate. One of the most useful things, therefore, that you can do is to review the actions of the play, in their proper order. In doing that, keep in mind that the play contains three distinct sorts of actions.

First, there are the events that took place before the time of the play and that are recounted on the stage. They are told not only for the benefit of the audience, but also for the players themselves. You will notice that many of these events are unknown to Oedipus as well as to the audience; hence the telling of them is more than a filling in of the spectators. Instead, it is one of the most important parts of the tragedy, for the ignorance of Oedipus concerning his parentage and concerning what he himself did, together with his coming to know the truth about these things, is what the tragedy is about.

Examples of this kind of event are what the messenger from Corinth tells about Polybus' death and about how he received the child Oedipus; so also the herdsman's tale which confirms that the child was indeed Iocasta's own. Oedipus himself supplies some very necessary background information—as when he recounts that in his youth in Corinth a drunken companion questioned his parentage. As a consequence, Oedipus consulted Apollo's oracle which warned him that he was fated to kill his father and marry his mother. In order to avoid this very fate, of course, Oedipus left Corinth and went to Thebes, thereby fulfilling the prophecy.

Secondly, there are the actions that take place right on the stage, before the spectators' eyes. This includes, of course, the *telling* of past events (especially as regards the reactions of the persons on the stage) as well as the events that take place for the first time, such as Oedipus' conversation with Teiresias, the blind soothsayer, and with Creon, his brother-in-law.

Whereas the past events that are recalled serve mainly to

inform Oedipus and the audience concerning *who* he is, the events that unfold before our eyes serve for the most part to reveal *what sort* of man he is. We see him react to various situations. His response, whatever else it may be, is always passionate: pity for the city of Thebes and its inhabitants, hatred for Teiresias, scorn for Creon.

Thirdly, there are some events that take place contemporaneously with the action on the stage, but are not shown to the audience. In *Oedipus the King* these are mainly Iocasta's suicide and Oedipus' multilation of himself.

The events that have a bearing on the play certainly cover a period of at least twenty years; they take place in a variety of locations. Yet the playwright has managed, through his skill, to let the events of these twenty years make themselves felt in the course of the play's action—during a time that can hardly exceed two hours, and all in one place, namely before the royal palace in Thebes. He can do that, obviously, only by *not* being a chronicler of twenty years in the life of Oedipus, but by being instead concerned with only one thing in Oedipus' life. That one thing, of course, is the discovery of who he is; all other events in and around the play have bearing only on that.

Oedipus' discovery of himself involves more than merely finding out who his parents were. It also involves showing him and the spectators what manner of man he is. He had a good opinion of himself; at the very beginning of the play, when he addresses the chorus of Theban Elders, he uses the expression "I, Oedipus renowned of all."

Part of his pride was no doubt due to having solved the riddle of the Sphinx. It was for this achievement that the Thebans made him king. According to legend the riddle was "What is four-footed in the morning, two-footed in the afternoon, and three-footed at evening?" The Thebans had to guess it, and whenever they failed, the Sphinx carried one of them off and devoured him. Oedipus guessed correctly that it was man; for the child crawls on hands and feet, the adult walks upright, and the old man supports his step with a stick. The

Sphinx then threw herself down from the mountain on which she dwelt.

In the concluding passage of the play the chorus refers to this achievement of Oedipus':

> Dwellers in our native Thebes, behold, this is Oedipus, who knew the famed riddle, and was a man most mighty; on whose fortunes what citizen did not gaze with envy? Behold into what a stormy sea of dread trouble he hath come!
>
> Therefore, while our eyes wait to see the destined final day, we must call no one happy who is of mortal race, until he hath crossed life's border, free from pain. (p. 113c)

III

Now let us turn to a few remarks of Aristotle about tragedy. We should try to see whether they are verified by our acquaintance with *Oedipus the King;* if they are, we should expect them to apply also to the *Antigone.* "We assume," Aristotle says,

> that, for the finest form of Tragedy, the Plot must be not simple but complex; and further, that it must imitate actions arousing fear and pity. . . .
>
> Three forms of plot are to be avoided. (1) A good man must not be seen passing from happiness to misery, or (2) a bad man from misery to happiness. The first situation is not fear-inspiring or piteous, but simply odious to us. The second is the most untragic that can be. . . . Nor . . . should (3) an extremely bad man be seen falling from happiness into misery. Such a story may arouse the human feeling in us, but it will not move us to either pity or fear; pity is occasioned by undeserved misfortune, and fear by that of one like ourselves; so that there will be nothing either piteous or fear-inspiring in the situation. There remains, then, the intermediate kind of personage, a man not preeminently virtuous and just, whose misfortune, however, is brought upon him not by vice or depravity but by some error in judgement, of the number of those in the enjoyment of great reputation and prosperity; e.g. Oedipus, Thyestes, and the men of note of similar families. (Vol. 9, p. 687c–d)

And one more remark of Aristotle's that may interest you as a reader of the drama:

> The Plot in fact should be so framed that, even without seeing the things take place, he who simply hears the account of them shall be

SOPHOCLES: *Oedipus* and *Antigone* 31

filled with horror and pity at the incidents; which is just the effect that the mere recital of the story in *Oedipus* would have on one. (Vol. 9, p. 688b)

IV

It is unfair to *Antigone* to read it in conjunction with *Oedipus the King*. It is almost certain to be compared with the other tragedy; and what should be considered as a superb tragedy in its own right will probably always suffer by comparison with *Oedipus the King*. Nevertheless, it meets all the criteria that Aristotle enumerates. It is, however, somewhat less unified than *Oedipus the King* and in some respects more complex.

For instance, it is hard to tell who the central character in the play is. Both Antigone and Creon qualify as tragic heroes. Both are of sufficiently grand stature, and both suffer from grievous flaws. Like her father, Oedipus, Antigone is possessed of a single-mindedness of purpose and a stubbornness that is both admirable and dangerous to its possessor. Indeed the chorus describes her as the "passionate child of passionate sire" and adds that she "knows not how to bend before troubles." Her passionate devotion to her duty leads her even to scorn her worthy sister whose temperament is softer and more prudent than her own.

Antigone's duty, as she sees it, is to bury her brother Polyneices who has been killed while waging war against his native Thebes. As a matter of fact, Eteocles, brother of both Antigone and Polyneices, killed Polyneices. Their uncle, Creon, the king of Thebes, forbids burial of Polyneices on the ground that he is a traitor, while Eteocles has an honorable funeral. But Antigone, to justify her actions, appeals to the supremacy of divine law over Creon's edict.

Yet Creon can by no means be made out as a monster. There is the indisputable fact that Polyneices tried to sack his native city, and that Antigone transgressed its law. That law may have been unjust and disapproved of by the gods; but we have only to remember Plato's *Crito* to realize that laws of any kind, and duty to one's country, impose a tremendous obligation on any citizen. And in the play itself there is a long speech by the chorus praising man and his works ("Wonders are many and none is more wonderful than man"); among these works is law which man must obey ("When he honours the laws of the land . . . proudly stands his city; no city hath he who, for his rashness, dwells with sin").

A further fact favorable to Creon is that, unlike Oedipus and Antigone, he realizes his mistake and tries to rectify it. But it is too late; and the end of the tragedy reveals a destruction as complete and as bloody as we see in *Oedipus the King*.

V

What is the crisis or turning point of Oedipus the King?

Aristotle, we saw, says that a tragedy should arouse pity and fear in the spectators. In Chapter 11 of *On Poetics*, he discusses two parts of the plot that tend to bring about these emotions. One is *reversal* of the hero's fortune; that is, some event that definitely starts the hero who is famous and prosperous on the road to suffering and misfortune. The other is *discovery*; this occurs when the hero finds out something important that causes a change within himself to correspond to the outward changes brought about by the reversal. In the best kind of tragedy, *reversal* and *discovery* go hand in hand. Thus Aristotle says:

> The finest form of Discovery is one attended by Peripeties [reversals], like that which goes with the Discovery in *Oedipus*. (Vol. 9, p. 687a)

What is the role of fate in a tragedy?

It is often said that tragic heros are fated to their doom; i.e., that they could not help what happened. This always seems somewhat unsatisfactory, since the mere unrolling of what must happen, without human agency, does not seem morally meaningful. If all of Oedipus' actions in the play are fated, how is he responsible for them, and how can his suffering and punishment be justified?

But what was Oedipus fated to do? According to the oracle, it was to kill his father and to marry his mother. Both of these events, however, have already taken place when the play opens. Fate, then, has already been fulfilled. What happens in the play itself, therefore, seems to be due to human agency.

Why is Teiresias, the seer, blind?

It is not, of course, Sophocles' invention to make the seer unseeing. He merely pictured Teiresias in the way that legend and tradition always had done. Yet Sophocles uses the device to perfection, contrasting Oedipus who has eyes but cannot see with Teiresias who is blind but sees. At the end of the play Oedipus is also blind; the question naturally arises: Can Oedipus now see?

Did Oedipus have genuine alternative courses of action open to him?

If he had not pressed the inquiry about the murderer of Laïus, he might have avoided the dreadful consequences. But was this an honorable possibility? The oracle demanded that in order to alleviate the plague the murderer be found. Oedipus was the king of Thebes. Hence it would seem to have been his duty to proceed with the inquiry.

Does this mean again that fate is the only causal agency in the play? Or is the necessity driving Oedipus of some other kind than fate?

Did Antigone have genuine alternative courses of action open to her?

Answering this question may also shed light on the previous one. There is no mention of any oracle in the *Antigone*. Yet what were her choices? Disobedience to the laws of her country or to divine laws. Was there a good choice possible between them? Do we, in our political and personal lives, have to make such choices? Are they always between evils, lesser and greater? What of the soldier who must perhaps kill the

innocent or himself be killed? Does this mean we cannot do or
be good in this life? Is there ever a third alternative—a good
alternative—to evil choices?

Who upholds justice—Creon or Antigone?

This question is closely related to the previous one. Consider what Antigone herself answers, when Creon asks her
"And thou didst indeed dare to transgress that law?"

> Antigone: Yes, for it was not Zeus that had published me that
> edict; not such are the laws set among men by the Justice who
> dwells with the gods below; nor deemed I that thy decrees were
> of such force, that a mortal could override the unwritten and un-
> failing statutes of heaven. For their life is not of to-day or yester-
> day, but from all time, and no man knows when they were first
> put forth.
>
> Not through dread of any human pride could I answer to the
> gods for breaking *these*. Die I must—I knew that well (how should
> I not?)—even without thy edicts. But if I am to die before my
> time, I count that a gain: for when any one lives, as I do, com-
> passed about with evils, can such an one find aught but gain in
> death? (p. 135a)

Why is it pleasurable to see tragedies performed?

Is there not something contradictory about associating
such dire events as are depicted in tragedies with pleasure?
Aristotle says that tragedy should arouse pity and fear in the
spectators. Why should that be considered pleasurable? Why
do we want to read or see tragedies?

The answer must involve some consideration of the kinds
of pleasure. It is clear, for instance, that enjoyment of comedy
and enjoyment of tragedy are of different kinds. Perhaps it
would not be wrong to say that the enjoyment of tragedy is
more intellectual than other pleasures. It certainly is not a
simple pleasure like a feeling of bodily well-being.

What is tragedy?

Is death a tragedy? Is it a greater tragedy than the one
Oedipus suffered? Is the death of an infant, of a very old man,
of an incurable sufferer tragic? Is the death of a patriotic hero

tragic? Is loss of friends, fortune, or reputation more or less tragic than death—or tragic at all?

These questions should be considered in connection with Aristotle's dicta on the nature and purpose of the tragedy. And remember that Aristotle is not talking about tragedy in real life, but about tragic *poetry*.

What makes a tragic hero?

Think of the modern tragedies you have read, or seen on the stage or in the movies, whose heroes are common men and women like ourselves. Are they tragic heroes or heroines of the same magnitude as the kings or queens who come to a tragic end in the Greek plays or in those of Shakespeare? Why or why not? And if tragedy is to evoke "pity and fear" in the spectator, as Aristotle tells us it should, how does the spectator identify himself with royalty (and thereby feel pity and fear)?

The following questions are designed to help you test the thoroughness of your reading. Each question is to be answered by giving a page or pages of the reading assignment. Answers will be found on page 189 of this Reading Plan.

1 What does Oedipus think is the reason for Teiresias' refusal to answer his question concerning the killer of Laïus?

2 How does Creon defend himself against Oedipus' charges?

3 How does Iocasta try to assuage Oedipus' dread of marrying his mother?

4 How did the Corinthian messenger receive Oedipus as a child?

5 Does Ismene condone her sister Antigone's actions?

6 Does Creon (in *Antigone*) follow Teiresias' advice?

7 How do Antigone and Haemon die?

ARISTOTLE

Nicomachean Ethics

Book I

Vol. 9, pp. 339–348

Happiness is the theme of the first book of Aristotle's *Nicomachean Ethics*. The fact that happiness is a subject of universal interest confirms Aristotle's most fundamental insight about it: all men want to be happy, and everything else they want they seek as a means of becoming happy. Among the things that men call good and strive for, happiness stands out as the one good which, if fully possessed, would leave a man satisfied and at rest. No one would call himself completely happy if anything essential to his well-being remained beyond his grasp. Happiness must, therefore, be the sum of all good things.

This, in brief, is the meaning of happiness that Aristotle sets before us, not as his own definition of it, but as the sense of it which everyone shares. Once we acknowledge this, as we must, we realize how often we misuse the word when we say, in a joyous moment, that we feel "happy" or, in a sad one, "unhappy." Life is full of good times and bad, moments of joy and sadness, but if happiness is the totality of goods, it cannot be found in one good time, or even in a lot of them, but only in a whole good life.

It is this fact about happiness which helps us to understand why the Declaration of Independence talks about the "pursuit of happiness" rather than the enjoyment of it as a natural human right. The pursuit of happiness takes a lifetime and only when the race has been run can we look back and say whether it has been well run or not. The first book of the *Nicomachean Ethics* proposes the standards by which we can judge whether or not it has.

Fourth Reading

I

It will be instructive to compare the first book of the *Nicomachean Ethics* with the first two books of Plato's *Republic*. Both are works dealing with morals or ethics; both contain their authors' best thought on these matters; and in both cases we read the introductory section.

In spite of these similarities, there are obvious and sharp differences between these two works. The first to come to mind, perhaps, is the difference in style. Whereas Plato's writing is always in the form of a dialogue, Aristotle's never is. Consequently, it usually is a little harder to discern what Plato's thought is on a given subject than Aristotle's. Plato never speaks to us in his own right but through the mouth of Socrates; and he usually chooses to present Socrates not as expounding a view, but rather as questioning others and extracting their point of view. In Aristotle's works, on the other hand, whatever their difficulty may be in other respects, it is never unclear that it is Aristotle who is talking and presenting his views.

However, after you have read several Platonic dialogues, you will find yourself developing an ability to see what is Plato's opinion on a given problem, in spite of the dialogue form. Aristotle certainly considered Plato as having an opinion on the subject of "good"; in Chapter 6 of the *Nicomachean Ethics*, he sets out to refute what he conceived the Platonic opinion on this point to be. The real difference, in other words, is not between dialogue and straight exposition, but between what these two works have to say.

Even prior to a detailed examination of the *Nicomachean Ethics*, we can indicate some of the differences and some of the similarities between it and *The Republic*.

1. Aristotle uses the question, "What is happiness?" as his introduction; whereas Plato uses the question, "What is justice?" as his beginning. We are probably safe in assuming that this is more than an accidental difference, and furthermore that it is an important one. An author is most likely to begin his moral treatise with that moral problem which he considers most important and not with some secondary question. Furthermore, Aristotle knew Plato's works; he knew that they contain no dialogue addressed to the question, "What is happiness?" Thus, the different beginning that Aristotle chooses for his moral treatise is no doubt deliberate.

2. Both Plato and Aristotle connect ethics very closely with politics. But the order of connection is different. Plato, as we saw, uses what is a political matter—the organization of the state—to explain a moral matter, viz., the nature of justice. Aristotle (as we shall see in the reading after this one) proceeds from ethics to politics.

3. Another difference derives almost directly from the differences in form. The *Nicomachean Ethics* is Aristotle's attempt to treat the subject of ethics in a systematic and complete fashion, insofar as that can be done by one philosopher. Plato's treatment, because of the dialogue form, is not systematic. Many more things are covered in the *Nicomachean Ethics* than in *The Republic*, for instance, the nature of courage, temperance, pleasure, friendship. Plato's omissions are only apparent, however, for these things are treated in other dialogues: *Laches* (courage); *Charmides* (temperance); *Philebus* (pleasure); *Lysis* (friendship).

4. The dialogue form means not only that the various ethical topics are distributed in various works of Plato; but also that any given dialogue is bound to be less simply organized than an expository treatise. Thus the *Nicomachean Ethics* has a much more readily apparent structure than *The Republic*; the mere division into books and chapters would

assure that. In this connection it is worth noting that Book I is, of course, an introductory book. Many topics touched on in it are taken up at greater length in Book II–X.

II

"Every art and every inquiry, and similarly every action and pursuit, is thought to aim at some good." This is how Aristotle begins the *Nicomachean Ethics;* and this sentence gives the key to the entire inquiry. For the subject of the treatise is the good; not the good of an art or an inquiry, but rather the good of action, and specifically human action. This, of course, is evident to us, when we say that the subject of the treatise is *ethics;* for ethics tells us what we ought to *do.*

In Chapter 2, Aristotle continues in this vein:

> If, then, there is some end of the things we do, which we desire for its own sake (everything else being desired for the sake of this), and if we do not choose everything for the sake of something else (for at that rate the process would go on to infinity, so that our desire would be empty and vain), clearly this must be the good and the chief good.

Almost at once the subject matter has been shown to be *the good*, or the greatest good. This follows if it is admitted that all human actions aim at some good. For unless there is a chief good at which ultimately all human actions aim, we cannot answer the question, "What is the aim of this action?" except by an infinite enumeration of goods, each one being desired for the sake of the next one. And that, as Aristotle says, would throw in doubt the desirability of the first action. For it is desirable because of some end, say A. But A is only desirable because of B, and B because of C, etc. And if this is an infinite series, its end can never be reached, and so any term of the series cannot be shown to be definitely desirable. For it is desirable only on the assumption of something that cannot be true, viz., that the end of the infinite series can be reached.

An example of this sort of thing would be a series of promissory notes, each based on someone else's promise to pay. For example, B promises to pay A $100, if C will pay B $100; and C says he will pay B $100, if D will pay him, C, $100, while D says that he will pay C $100, if only E will pay him, D, $100, etc. It is clear that A will never get his $100 unless somebody pays up unconditionally in this series, i.e., without making his payment conditional on someone else's payment. If the series of promises, therefore, is infinite, A will never get his $100. In this sense the chief good is an unconditional good—its goodness is not based on the goodness of something else.

The next question naturally is what this greatest good is. Aristotle raises it in Chapter 4:

> Let us resume our inquiry and state, in view of the fact that all knowledge and every pursuit aims at some good . . . what is the highest of all goods achievable by action. Verbally there is very general agreement; for both the general run of men and people of superior refinement say that it is happiness. . . .

But that this agreement is only verbal is clear at once, and Aristotle adds "with regard to what happiness is they differ, and the many do not give the same account as the wise."

Aristotle returns to the question of happiness in Chapter 7 and discusses what sort of thing it must be. "Not all ends are final ends;" he says, "but the chief good is evidently something final . . . and therefore we call final without qualification that which is always desirable in itself and never for the sake of something else." He continues:

> Now such a thing happiness, above all else, is held to be; for this we choose always for itself and never for the sake of something else, but honour, pleasure, reason, and every virtue we choose indeed for themselves (for if nothing resulted from them we should still choose each of them), but we choose them also for the sake of happiness, judging that by means of them we shall be happy. Happiness, on the other hand, no one chooses for the sake of these, nor, in general, for anything other than itself.
>
> From the point of view of self-sufficiency the same result seems to follow; for the final good is thought to be self-sufficient. . . . The self-sufficient we now define as that which when isolated makes life desirable and lacking in nothing; and such we think

happiness to be. . . . Happiness, then, is something final and self-sufficient, and is the end of action. (pp. 342d–343a)

We may be tempted to consider the last sentence as a definition of happiness, but Aristotle is still dissatisfied, since he begins the next paragraph thus: "Presumably, however, to say that happiness is the chief good seems a platitude. . . ." He sets out to give a non-platitudinous definition of it, by considering that the good of anything that has a function resides in that function. For instance, the good of the hammer resides in its function, hammering. Thus, the good of the hammer is to drive nails, and to do this well. And in turn the good of the carpenter lies in performing well *his* function. What is the function of *man?* This becomes the crucial question for the determination of man's good and his chief good.

The determination of man's function is made in a very compact paragraph on page 343a–c. Here let us merely record Aristotle's conclusion:

> We state the function of man to be a certain kind of life, and this to be an activity or actions of the soul implying a rational principle, and the function of a good man to be the good and noble performance of these, and if any action is well performed when it is performed in accordance with the appropriate excellence: if this is the case, human good turns out to be activity of soul in accordance with virtue, and if there are more than one virtue, in accordance with the best and most complete.

In both of the last quotations, Aristotle places great emphasis on the notion of *completeness.* "Happiness is something final and self-sufficient . . ." and "human good [is] activity of soul . . . in accordance with the best and most complete [virtue]."

The crucial aspect of happiness is just this sufficiency and completeness. He who has it is "lacking in nothing." And so Aristotle sums up his discussion of happiness in the following paragraph.

> He is happy who is active in accordance with complete virtue and is sufficiently equipped with external goods, not for some chance period but throughout a complete life. Or must we add 'and who

is destined to live thus and dies as befits his life'? Certainly the future is obscure to us, while happiness, we claim, is an end and something in every way final. If so, we shall call happy those among living men in whom these conditions are, and are to be, fulfilled—but happy *men*. (p. 346c)

For Aristotle, therefore, the happy man leads a *good life*, he is not a man who has a *good time*. Having a good time, though often desirable and not necessarily bad, is a passing thing. It is a feeling of pleasure, and like all feelings or emotions it lacks just that quality of stability and sufficiency that marks happiness.

Happiness, in other words, is a moral quality for Aristotle, involving *all* virtues and all of a lifetime. Just because it is such a complete and completely satisfying thing, it is also hard to achieve; only the virtuous man can hope to attain it.

III

Why does Aristotle restrict his definition of happiness to men, as he does in the last phrase of the last quotation?

Whom or what does Aristotle wish to exclude from this definition of happiness? Does it not fit beings higher than man (if there are any), such as gods, or does it not fit animals? Presumably the answer is that this definition of happiness does not fit either higher or lower beings than man. But why not? Perhaps it is easy to see that the chief good of brute animals is different from that of man; but why is the chief good of a god different from man's?

What is the role of external goods in happiness?

Aristotle's happiness is not an ascetic one. He does not maintain that a destitute and sick man can be as happy as one who is materially and physically well off. This is especially interesting if we remember that happiness is an activity of the soul involving reason. It is sometimes supposed that thinking and being a philosopher are "other-worldly" occupations and that a person following them will reject all worldly goods. But this is clearly not Aristotle's view. Evidently, the happy man must have his share of each of the various kinds of goods.

Why does happiness involve "a complete life"?

You may remember that the last line of *Oedipus the King* goes like this:

> We must call no one happy who is of mortal race, until he hath crossed life's border, free from pain.

Aristotle similarly refers to a like saying of Solon's. You may want to read the story of Solon and Croesus as Herodotus tells it, in Volume 6, pages 6c–8a, and its conclusion, pages 20b–21a.

But why would Aristotle object to calling someone sometimes happy, and sometimes unhappy? Why, in other words, is happiness not the sort of thing that comes and goes? If no one can be called happy until he is dead, we shall never be able to say that any one *is* happy; at best we can say of a dead person that he *was* happy.

What is the role of pleasure in happiness?

Pleasure is not one of the external goods which Aristotle says the happy man must have. Does this mean, then, that the happy life is not pleasant? This seems hardly a defensible view. On the contrary, most people would probably identify happiness with pleasure. Aristotle mentions this view in Chapter 5:

> To judge from the lives that men lead, most men, and men of the most vulgar type, seem (not without some ground) to identify the good, or happiness, with pleasure. (p. 340d)

However, he returns to the consideration of pleasure in Chapter 8 of Book I. Although in Chapter 5 he denies that pleasure is the chief good or happiness, in Chapter 8 he assigns to pleasure a place in the happy life.

SELF-TESTING QUESTIONS

The following questions are designed to help you test the thoroughness of your reading. Each question is to be answered by giving a page or pages of the reading assignment. Answers will be found on page 189 of this Reading Plan.

1 Why is ethics not an exact science?

2 Does Aristotle think that a child can be happy?

3 How does Aristotle distinguish between happiness and blessedness?

4 Is a young person a proper student of ethics?

5 How does Aristotle divide the kinds of goods?

6 What are the kinds of life that Aristotle considers as candidates for the happy life?

7 What are the two parts of the irrational element of the soul?

ARISTOTLE

Politics

Book I

Vol. 9, pp. 445–455

We live under a constitutional form of government. We are, as citizens, constituent members of the State and its ruling class. No man is our political superior: those who hold the offices of state are our representatives, chosen by our suffrage. We are thus free men and equals. In other countries, where the reign of constitutional law is unknown and no one is a citizen, the despotic power wielded by some men subjugates the rest.

The blessings of political liberty and equality, which we so often take for granted, are the gift of two great inventions for which we are indebted to the ancient Greeks—*constitutions* and *citizenship*. In the whole history of political thought and action, there are no ideas more revolutionary than these. Aristotle's *Politics* is the first full statement of the theory of these two ideas. Its opening book repeatedly calls our attention to the fundamental difference in the condition of those who, on the one hand, live as slaves or as the subjects of despotic kings and those who, on the other hand, live as citizens under constitutional governments and who, therefore, are "free men and equals, ruling and being ruled in turn."

In Aristotle's conception, the *polis*—which is the Greek word for state—does not come into existence until men *constitute* the government under which they live. Since, in his view, man is by nature a *political* animal (which means that man is intended by nature to be a *constituent* of the state), he asks us to be grateful to those men who first constituted the state. They are, he says, "the greatest of benefactors." We owe them the blessings of the citizenship we enjoy.

Fifth Reading

I

In the usual arrangement of Aristotle's works the *Politics* follows immediately after the *Nicomachean Ethics;* it is, in fact, a continuation of it. The last chapter of the last book of the *Nicomachean Ethics* has Aristotle telling us why he is not finished with his treatment of moral matters, and why he goes on to write a political work.

"If these matters and the virtues, and also friendship and pleasure, have been dealt with sufficiently in outline," he asks,

> are we to suppose that our programme has reached its end? Surely . . . where there are things to be done the end is not to survey and recognize the various things, but rather to do them; with regard to virtue, then, it is not enough to know, but we must try to have and use it, or try any other way there may be of becoming good. (p. 434a–b)

Hence the next thing to be discussed must be how to become virtuous. "But," he says a little later, "it is difficult to get from youth up a right training for virtue if one has not been brought up under right laws." (p. 434c) And again he adds,

> surely he who wants to make men . . . better by his care must try to become capable of legislating, if it is through laws that we can become good. (p. 435c)

And so he begins the final paragraph of the *Nicomachean Ethics* as follows:

> Now our predecessors have left the subject of legislation to us unexamined; it is perhaps best, therefore, that we should ourselves study it, and in general study the question of the constitution, in

order to complete to the best of our ability our philosophy of human nature. (p. 436c)

This sets the stage for the *Politics:* we must learn about the state and about legislation because it is in this way that men become virtuous.

The first book of the *Politics* has a much clearer structure than the first book of the *Nicomachean Ethics.* We find it divided into three main parts.

First, we have Chapters 1 and 2, having to do with the origin and nature of the state.

Secondly, the section from Chapter 3 through Chapter 7. This is devoted to the subject of slavery.

Thirdly, the remaining chapters (8 through 13). These constitute a small and self-contained treatise on economics. (Household management, which is the term that the translator here uses, is the literal meaning of the Greek word *oikonomia,* from which *economics* is derived.)

We shall say a few words about each of these sections.

II

In the first sentence of Chapter 2, Aristotle indicates the method he is going to use in his investigation of the state:

> He who thus considers things in their first growth and origin, whether a state or anything else, will obtain the clearest view of them. (p. 445b–c)

It is evidently a generally applicable method in Aristotle's view: it tries to discover the nature of things by tracing how they came to be. It is therefore often called the "genetic method"; we might also call it a "biological method," since it treats the state as though it grew like a living thing.

As any growing thing has different stages, so Aristotle considers the several stages that preceded the fully developed state.

> In the first place there must be a union of those who cannot exist without each other; namely, of male and female, that the race

may continue (and this is a union which is formed, not of deliberate purpose, but because, in common with other animals and with plants, mankind have a natural desire to leave behind them an image of themselves), and of natural ruler and subject, that both may be preserved. (p. 445c)

Notice that Aristotle in this passage speaks of two things as natural: first, the desire for procreation, and second, the relation of ruler and subject. We shall come back to the topic of what is "natural" shortly. For the present, let us continue to follow the genesis of the state.

Out of these two relationships between man and woman, master and slave, the first thing to arise is the family. . . . The family is the association established by nature for the supply of men's everyday wants. . . . (p. 445d)

Notice that again the family is said to be established "by nature." Several families now unite into a village, and we are ready for the last step:

When several villages are united in a single complete community, large enough to be nearly or quite self-sufficing, the state comes into existence, originating in the bare needs of life, and continuing in existence for the sake of a good life. (p. 446a)

Now we see why Aristotle kept calling attention to what is natural or "by nature"; for he continues this way:

Therefore, if the earlier forms of society are natural, so is the state, for it is the end of them, and the nature of a thing is its end. For what each thing is when fully developed, we call its nature, whether we are speaking of a man, a horse, or a family. (p. 446b)

What is the sense in which Aristotle uses the word "natural"? There are clearly several different notes in its meaning. From the example of the union of male and female, we may infer that a natural event does not depend on human deliberation, for Aristotle contrasts what happens by "deliberate purpose" with what happens from "natural desire." Furthermore, we may infer that a natural event is one that takes place always or nearly always. Male and female plants and animals always—or for the most part—unite to procreate. Those who do not are the exception.

Related to the non-deliberate character of the natural event is the fact that a natural thing is contrasted with an artificial one. An artificial thing comes to be as the result of art—and hence of human deliberation and purpose. A natural thing, on the other hand, comes to be simply because of what it is, or because of its nature.

And the nature of each thing, Aristotle has already said, "is what each thing is when fully developed." So it is this —the fully developed thing—which is, as it were, responsible for the thing developing in the way it does. We can illustrate this in the case of a living being, say an animal. What a cat is going to be when fully developed governs the development of the kitten—everything is oriented toward this.

Now let us see what it means to call the state natural, and to say that "man is by nature a political animal." First, the state arises out of a human need, just as the family arises out of the human need for procreation and protection of the young. Indeed, we have already quoted Aristotle as saying that "the state comes into existence, originating in the bare needs of life; and continuing in existence for the sake of a good life." Secondly, all men are meant to live in a state. Life without a state is primitive and not as good as in the state. "A social instinct," Aristotle says,

> is implanted in all men by nature, and yet he who first founded the state was the greatest of benefactors. For man, when perfected, is the best of animals, but, when separated from law and justice, he is the worst of all; since armed injustice is the more dangerous, and he is equipped at birth with arms, meant to be used by intelligence and virtue, which he may use for the worst ends. Wherefore, if he have not virtue, he is the most unholy and the most savage of animals, and the most full of lust and gluttony. But justice is the bond of men in states, for the administration of justice, which is the determination of what is just, is the principle of order in political society. (p. 446d)

Thirdly, if the state is natural, then what it is and how it comes to be cannot be completely due to human deliberation and rules. Men do not determine what the state is and what it does, in the same way in which the sculptor determines what the statue is and does. This means that the picture of the *Republic* is fanciful; no utopian state can be brought into being.

Fourthly, since the state is a natural thing, it has an end or purpose. That is to say, it is not some chance aggregation of people, as a heap of stones is a chance aggregation of stones. The state exists for the sake of the good life.

> If all communities aim at some good, the state or political community, which is the highest of all, and which embraces all the rest, aims at good in a greater degree than any other, and at the highest good. (p. 445a)

III

We have made much of the *naturalness* of the state; but the notion of the natural is even more important in the second section of Book I. Here we deal with slavery. "A slave," Aristotle says, is "an instrument of action." But, though an instrument, he is "a human being [and] also a possession." (end of chap. 4, p. 447c)

And just because the slave is human, he can do things that no inanimate instrument yet invented can do.

> For if every instrument could accomplish its own work, obeying or anticipating the will of others . . . if, in like manner, the shuttle would weave and the plectrum touch the lyre without a hand to guide them, chief workmen would not want servants, nor masters slaves. (p. 447b–c)

Thus Aristotle here envisages not only mechanization, but even what we nowadays call "automation"; if it existed, he says, menial or slavish work would be done away with, and consequently also the need for servants and slaves. Thus Aristotle also clearly saw what people now both hope and fear from automation: the hope is for the elimination of dull, servile, and slavish work; the fear is that workers will be eliminated together with the work.

Aristotle, however, not only speaks of *work* that is by its nature slavish; he also speaks of *men* that are by their nature slavish. And this must be appreciated in its full force: Aristotle does not mean simply that some men are better suited for menial jobs; he means to say that by nature some men are and ought to be slaves—another man's possessions.

Already, in Chapter 2, when discussing the origin of the state, Aristotle hints at what is to come. He speaks of the "union of those who cannot exist without each other"; these unions are between male and female, and between "natural ruler and subject, that both may be preserved." He goes on:

> For that which can foresee by the exercise of mind is by nature intended to be lord and master, and that which can with its body give effect to such foresight is a subject, and by nature a slave; hence master and slave have the same interest. (p. 445c)

From the point of view of justifying slavery, the last clause is the most important. Ordinarily, we tend to think that the interest of the slave is opposite to that of the master. The slave wants to be free, we imagine, and wants to be able to do what he wishes instead of serving the needs of the master. Aristotle, however, here envisages a situation where it serves both the slave and the master to have the master be master and the slave be slave. This becomes even more explicit in Chapter 5, when Aristotle asks, "Is there any one intended by nature to be a slave, and for whom such a condition is expedient and right, or rather is not all slavery a violation of nature?"

"There is no difficulty in answering this question," he continues, but the answer he gives sounds strange to twentieth-century ears:

> That some should rule and others be ruled is a thing not only necessary, but expedient; from the hour of their birth, some are marked out for subjection, others for rule. (p. 447d)

We need only to recall the words of the Declaration of Independence to realize we are in unfamiliar territory:

> We hold these truths to be self-evident, that all men are created equal; that they are endowed by their Creator with certain un-

alienable rights; that among these are life, liberty, and the pursuit of happiness. (Vol. 43, p. 1a)

How does Aristotle justify slavery? He says that slavery is natural, and denies that all men are equal. He finds a difference of nature among men, of such a sort that for some men it is natural to be masters, while for others it is natural to be slaves.

> Where then there is such a difference as that between soul and body, or between men and animals (as in the case of those whose business is to use their body, and who can do nothing better), the lower sort are by nature slaves, and it is better for them as for all inferiors that they should be under the rule of a master. For he who can be, and therefore is, another's, and he who participates in rational principle enough to apprehend, but not to have, such a principle, is a slave by nature.

Yet the slave is still a man, not an animal:

> the lower animals cannot even apprehend a principle; they obey their instincts. (p. 448b)

Here the question of automation arises again, and we may consider the limits—if any—of the potentialities of the machine and the differences between machines and men, on the one hand, and between the human and the non-human instrument (or between the natural slave and the machine), on the other. What kind of things which human beings can do, will machines never be able to do because the tasks or processes are not mechanical? Will machines, for example, even the flexible calculators that we have come to call "thinking machines," ever be able to think, to consider ideas, to criticize things, to invent or create anything? Aristotle's natural slave is able to apprehend principles; the lower animals obey their instincts; but inanimate instruments do neither.

Two questions remain to be asked of Aristotle here. First, are there really any natural slaves? Secondly, what are we to say when someone who is not by nature a slave is nevertheless enslaved as the result of war or captivity? Both of these questions are, of course, as relevant to modern times as to ancient, and especially to the modern doctrine of "racial superiority," held either on the grounds of nature or on the grounds of mere power over an "inferior" group.

Aristotle does not directly answer the first question. His argument above, you will notice, is couched in hypothetical terms: "Where there is a man of this sort, then he ought to be a slave." Hence we may say for him that if there are no such men—men of this lower nature—then there can be no natural slavery. It is probably a fair assumption, however, that Aristotle must have believed that there are natural slaves; it is hard to imagine he would have devoted so much space to a merely hypothetical situation.

The second question is directly answered by Aristotle. Legal, or conventional, slavery does occur; and slavery that is not based on nature is unjust. This topic is discussed in Chapter 6.

IV

The last section of the book, dealing with economics, is also of great interest. Much of it is still valuable today, beyond being historically significant as the first treatment of the subject. Karl Marx, in *Capital*, refers to this section of the *Politics* several times with approval. (You can find the places where he does, by looking in the index to *Capital*, Vol. 50, pp. 395 ff.)

Here we have only space to point out that once more the notion of the natural plays a crucial role. Just as there was a natural as well as a conventional slavery, so here Aristotle distinguishes between a natural art of wealth-getting and an artificial kind. Wealth-getting that is natural is part of the management of the household

> in so far as the art of household management must either find ready to hand, or itself provide, such things necessary to life, and useful for the community of the family or state, as can be stored. . . . But there is a boundary fixed, just as there is in other arts; for the instruments of any art are never unlimited, either in number or size, and riches may be defined as a number of instruments to be used in a household or in a state. (p. 450d)

The essential notion of this natural art of wealth-getting is its limitation; wealth is merely an instrument and is not to be acquired for its own sake. Evidently in Aristotle's times there were men who thought otherwise:

> There is another variety of the art of acquisition which is commonly and rightly called an art of wealth-getting, and has in fact suggested the notion that riches and property have no limit. . . . The kind already described is given by nature, the other is gained by experience and art.

Aristotle disapproves of the art of wealth-getting without limit and the men who practice it:

> Some persons are led to believe that getting wealth is the object of household management, and the whole idea of their lives is that they ought either to increase their money without limit, or at any rate not to lose it. The origin of this disposition in men is that they are intent upon living only, and not upon living well; and, as their desires are unlimited, they also desire that the means of gratifying them should be without limit. (p. 452a)

From this we see some additional notes in the meaning of "natural" as Aristotle uses it. It involves the notion of limitation, and being directed toward the right end. By contrast, the unnatural is boundless and misguided. And thus naturalness clearly has moral implications for Aristotle: the natural art of wealth-getting is good; the unnatural art is not.

In general, Aristotle's discussion in this book seems to be directed by the consideration of what is natural. Because of the specific nature of man—man is by nature a political animal—life in a state is natural and good for men. Because of their individual natures, some men are natural rulers and others natural slaves. Because of the nature of the household, there is a natural art of wealth-getting and its pursuit is good and honorable.

V

Is the genetic method appropriate to an investigation of the state?

After all, the state is not a living thing; why then should a method that treats it like one be successful? It may be misleading, for there are definite differences between a natural living thing and a state. For instance, though Aristotle speaks of the state as natural, even he would admit that it is also in part artificial, i.e., the deliberate work of men. It does not grow from seed as a plant does. Though it is natural for men to associate in a state, this association does not take place without their doing something about it. As a matter of fact, men almost always *do* do something about it—a sign that the state is in fact natural.

What is the meaning of "natural," as Aristotle uses the term?

Considering that so much depends on the term, Aristotle is pretty casual about it in this book. "What each thing is when fully developed, we call its nature" he says at one point. This seems to identify the thing with its nature. But at other times, the nature of a thing seems to be what it ought to be, or what it is going to be. And at still other times, nature appears to be personified, as when Aristotle speaks of "the intentions of nature."

Aristotle says that the soul rules the body despotically, and that the intellect rules the appetites with a constitutional and royal rule. Is this to be taken literally?

In what sense can Aristotle be talking of ruling here? After all, he cannot mean to personify body and soul to the extent that the soul addresses commands to the body, or the intellect to the passions. These remarks about ruling occur in the chapter where the natural slave is discussed (chap. 5). Is the body the natural slave of the soul? But do we not speak of the body enslaving the soul or higher parts of man sometimes?

What does it mean to call man a political animal?

Why does Aristotle emphasize the "animal"? He refers to

other social or gregarious animals such as bees and ants. In what sense is man alone "political"? Elsewhere Aristotle calls man a rational animal. Is there any relation between man's political and his rational nature? Does it make sense to call the state not only a natural human institution, but also a rational institution? Is the state, in other words, a work of reason? Or is it a work of passion, in the sense that men's mutual enmity and hatred force them to band together, lest they all kill each other?

What is the role of property in the state?

Evidently it must be an important role: for the state comes to be out of the village, and the village out of the family. The family again counts among its members slaves. But slaves are possessions or property, and so Aristotle is led to talk about the management of property. Even aside from the existence of slaves, however, the fact that Aristotle devotes so much time to household management shows how important he considers the subject. And unless there were property—private property—there would be nothing to manage in a household. That is why, for example, the guardians in *The Republic* need not know anything about the management of property. It is no part of their education, for they have neither households nor private property.

We can also see how important private property is, according to Aristotle, in the following way. The state is natural, being made up of natural units, namely families. But if the family is a natural unit, then everything that goes into making it must be natural. And property is one of the things that is required in order to maintain the family as a unit. Without it, the family would fall back on charity from the state and would lose its identity as a group. This is why, in the theory of the Communist state—not just Plato's *The Republic*, but Marx's and Lenin's—the family plays a non-existent or insignificant role. In practice, as we see it in the Soviet Union, the family persists and so do some forms of private property.

What is the relation—in Aristotle and in actual lives with which you are acquainted—between the goods of fortune (such as money, fame, and power) and happiness?

The hard problem here is not the theoretical validity of Aristotle's doctrine, but its "salability." Most men seem now —and always—to pursue the lesser or incomplete goods, goods which fortune distributes capriciously, at the sacrifice of greater goods, and especially those which can be won by virtue. Perhaps Aristotle is fundamentally wrong about human nature. How shall we set about determining this? And what would follow, for ethics, politics, the family, and the state, if we conclude that Aristotle was wrong and that men by nature are inclined to seek money, fame, and power instead of virtue?

Are there in fact "natural" and "unnatural" arts of money-making?

The Christian church, holding that usury is sinful, for centuries discouraged the practice of moneylending at interest, that is, of banking. Aristotle seems to take the same view of "begetting money by money." Here again we encounter a profound problem regarding human nature and the place that the desire for gain *for the sake of gain* holds in it. The fable of King Midas may be useful to consider here, or the condition of Dickens' Ebenezer Scrooge. But does their fate befall all who love money? And why does Jesus call it the root of all evil, and make it harder for the rich man to enter heaven than for a camel to pass through a needle's eye?

The following questions are designed to help you test the thoroughness of your reading. Each question is to be answered by giving a page or pages of the reading assignment. Answers will be found on page 190 of this Reading Plan.

1 What are Aristotle's arguments for saying that the state is prior to the family?

2 What are the three relations in the family?

3 When are master and slave friends, and when are they enemies?

4 What are the two uses to which anything may be put?

5 What is the least honorable method of wealth-getting, according to Aristotle?

6 How did Thales make himself rich?

7 Does a slave have any virtue?

PLUTARCH

The Lives of the Noble Grecians and Romans

Vol. 14, "Lycurgus," "Numa Pompilius,"
"Lycurgus and Numa Compared," pp. 32–64;
"Alexander," "Caesar," pp. 540–604

The drawing of comparisons is an exercise which delights the human mind. We somehow feel that we understand things better when we have a lively perception of their similarities and differences. This is particularly true in the field of history. We understand our own country better by comparing it with other countries, or our own century by comparing it with other centuries. And when we compare nations or epochs, we inevitably consider the great men or the leaders who represent or symbolize their outstanding achievements.

Most of us, for example, thinking back on recent history, cannot help being fascinated by the contrasting figures of Woodrow Wilson and Lloyd George in World War I, or those of Franklin D. Roosevelt and Winston Churchill in World War II. These were the great men of their day and, in our judgment, they were good men, too. But we are no less fascinated by great men who are not good men. A comparison of the greatness—and badness—of Benito Mussolini, Adolf Hitler, and Joseph Stalin is, if anything, more interesting and instructive.

Plutarch is not just an ordinary writer of biography. He is uniquely the writer of comparisons which give us the liveliest understanding of ancient Greece and Rome. The men he compares are the great ones of their day—the great *bad* ones as well as the great *good* ones. In his parallel lives and comparison of Numa and Lycurgus, we have two great benefactors of mankind —two lawgivers. In his treatment of Alexander and Caesar, we have two great conquerors and ruthless seekers after power. And, there presenting us with their parallel lives, he leaves the comparison for us to draw.

Sixth Reading

I

People are interested in people, and Plutarch wrote about people. The *Lives* is one of those books with which almost everyone is familiar, even if he has never read any of it. The familiarity extends beyond the mere name, since much of what is in Plutarch has found its way into other books or even into our general knowledge of antiquity.

For instance, in reading the life of Alexander you will come across the famous story of the Gordian knot—the knot which was so complicated that no one had been able to untie it. Similarly, you may be familiar with stories about the mathematician Archimedes; if you were to read the life of Marcellus, you would there (pp. 252a–255a) find the account of how Archimedes almost singlehandedly staved off the siege of Syracuse with his elaborate machines. In the same place, there is the story of how Archimedes was killed by a Roman soldier, while he was engrossed in a mathematical problem.

Still another way in which Plutarch's *Lives* have become a traditional part of the thought of English-speaking peoples is through the plays of Shakespeare. An English translation of the *Lives* by Sir Thomas North first appeared in 1579, and formed the source for Shakespeare's Roman plays, *Julius Caesar, Coriolanus,* and *Antony and Cleopatra.*

Plutarch wrote many other works beside the *Lives.* They are usually grouped together under the common name of *Opera moralia* or *Moral Works.* They include such essays as *On the Education of Children, On Virtue and Vice, Advice to the Married,* and many others. All have been translated into English. The present translation of the *Lives*, though commonly called the Dryden translation, was actually made by a number of persons at the end of the seventeenth century. Dryden contributed only a life of Plutarch and his name to the edition, no doubt in order to make it seem more attractive to prospective purchasers.

Not too much is known about Plutarch's own life; his dates are usually given as A.D. 46–120, though this is only approximate. But it is definite that he lived and wrote during the period that Gibbon called the golden age of the Roman Empire; the latter part of his life was spent during the reigns of Nerva, Trajan, and perhaps Hadrian. This is of interest because it means that Plutarch's work is not what we might call "propaganda." At least his immediate purpose is *not* to deplore the present state of affairs and to praise the past, in order to arouse the citizens to return to the ways of their forefathers. This is not to deny that the *Lives* often read as though Plutarch thinks that the men he writes about are better than his contemporaries. But their superiority is a moral one —customs and manners were better in the old days. It was simply not possible in the days of Trajan to think that Roman might could ever have been greater than it was then. This helps to explain why Plutarch's writings are moral rather than political in character. Another contributing factor is that Plutarch himself was not a Roman but a Greek. The time of Greek military power was long past and the influence of Greece was now exclusively cultural. Building and protecting an empire was a Roman, not a Greek, worry.

Plutarch was born at Chaeronea in Boeotia; he was trained in Athens and spent some time in Rome. But he lived for the most part and died in his native city. There he held both political and priestly offices. He had at least five children; one of them was a daughter who died young. Plutarch, who was not present at the child's death, wrote a long letter to his wife Timoxena, trying to strengthen and encourage her. Under the title *Consolation to His Wife,* this letter has been preserved.

II

Plutarch's fame, of course, rests mainly on his biographical work. He insists that the biographer's task is different from that of the historian. Consequently the *Lives* are less concerned to be factually complete than to emphasize and illustrate a few points judged to be important by Plutarch. Usually these points are moral in nature.

> It must be borne in mind that my design is not to write histories, but lives. And the most glorious exploits do not always furnish us with the clearest discoveries of virtue or vice in men; sometimes a matter of less moment, an expression or a jest, informs us better of their characters and inclinations, than the most famous sieges, the greatest armaments, or the bloodiest battles whatsoever. Therefore, as portrait-painters are more exact in the lines and features of the face, in which the character is seen, than in the other parts of the body, so I must be allowed to give my more particular attention to the marks and indications of the souls of men, and while I endeavour by these to portray their lives, may be free to leave more weighty matters and great battles to be treated of by others. (540d–541a)

Fifteen hundred years later, we find Montaigne, one of the greatest admirers of Plutarch, agreeing with him. In an essay entitled "On the Education of Children" Montaigne advocates reading Plutarch for the sake of moral training (see Vol. 25, p. 68c–d):

> What profit shall [a boy] not reap as to the business of men, by reading the lives of Plutarch? But, withal, let my governor remember to what end his instructions are principally directed, and that he do not so much imprint in his pupil's memory the date of the ruin of Carthage, as the manners of Hannibal and Scipio; nor so much where Marcellus died, as why it was unworthy of his duty that he died there. Let him not teach him so much the narrative parts of history as to judge them. . . . There are in Plutarch many long discourses very worthy to be carefully read and observed, for he is, in my opinion, of all others the greatest master in that kind of writing. . . . Plutarch had rather we should applaud his judgment than commend his knowledge, and had rather leave us with an appetite to read more, than glutted with that we have already read.

And another two hundred years later, we read in Immanuel Kant similar praise for the reading of biographies, though he does not mention Plutarch by name:

> I do not know why the educators of youth have not long since made use of this propensity of reason to enter with pleasure upon the most subtle examination of the practical questions that are thrown up; and why they have not, after first laying the foundation of a purely moral catechism, searched through the biographies of ancient and modern times with the view of having at hand instances of the duties laid down, in which, especially by comparison of similar actions under different circumstances, they might exercise the critical judgement of their scholars in remarking their greater or less moral significance.

This passage occurs near the very end of the *Critique of Practical Reason* (Vol. 42, p. 357c–d). A few lines later, Kant has some words of criticism:

> Only I wish they [the educators] would spare them [their pupils] the example of so-called *noble* (super-meritorious) actions, in which our sentimental books so much abound, and would refer all to duty merely, and to the worth that a man can and must give himself in his own eyes by the consciousness of not having transgressed it, since whatever runs up into empty wishes and longings after inaccessible perfection produces mere heroes of romance, who, while they pique themselves on their feeling for transcendent greatness, release themselves in return from the observance of common and every-day obligations, which then seem to them petty and insignificant.

Down the ages critics have agreed that the *Lives* is a book of moral instruction. It is therefore appropriate to compare it with other works of morality. If you look back on the earlier readings in this series, you will find that they can all be characterized as (at least in part) works in the field of morals. But they differ widely in their form: We have had a public speech (*Apology*), dialogues (*Crito* and *The Republic*), plays (*Oedipus the King* and *Antigone*), straight exposition (*Nicomachean Ethics* and *Politics*), and now biography. The long quotation from Montaigne makes clear that moral matters may also be treated in essay form; furthermore, it is apparent that historical narrative can be (again at least partly) moral in import. It may surprise you, however, to learn that at least one moral work, Spinoza's *Ethics* (see Vol. 31), is written, like geometry, in the form of axioms, definitions, and demonstrations.

This wide diversity in form naturally raises the question whether all these forms or styles are equally suitable for writing about moral matters, or whether these differences in form are correlated with some difference in content. At least in the case of the biographical form, the answer seems clear. Biographies necessarily deal with particular events and men; they do not develop moral principles as such, though they may illustrate them. The biographical form, then, seems most suited for a particular purpose, viz., that of instructing by way of example; and especially of instructing young people in moral matters.

III

In addition to being a biographer, is Plutarch also a historian?

To make this question more concrete, we may ask ourselves whether Plutarch, in addition to writing the life of Caesar, also writes the history of Rome during Caesar's lifetime. The answer must probably be both affirmative and negative.

Since Plutarch's subjects are always noble and famous men, what they did and what happened to them invariably affected the course of events. Much of Rome's history during Caesar's lifetime is, in other words, identical with Caesar's life. Yet, on the other hand, the perspective of the historian would be different from that of the biographer. The former would focus his attention on Rome, the latter on Caesar. The biographer, therefore, includes details that the historian omits, and the historian finds many things relevant to his subject which the biographer slights or ignores.

Is biography more akin to history or to poetry?

The following quotation is from Aristotle's *On Poetics;* it may help you with your answer:

> The poet's function is to describe, not the thing that has happened, but a kind of thing that might happen, i.e., what is possible as being probable or necessary. The distinction between historian and poet is not in the one writing prose and the other verse—you might put the work of Herodotus into verse, and it would still be a species of history; it consists really in this, that the one describes the thing that has been, and the other a kind of thing that might be. Hence poetry is something more philosophic and of graver import than history, since its statements are of the nature rather of universals, whereas those of history are singulars. (Vol. 9, p. 686a)

On the basis of what point or points did Plutarch compare Alexander and Caesar?

There are certainly obvious similarities between the two men: both were excellent generals; their fame lasted and was perhaps never surpassed; both were important statesmen as well as generals; both were very liberal to their friends. No doubt other points of similarity can be found.

But equally impressive is the list of differences between them; and this raises the problem of whether they are suitably compared. Note some of the differences: Alexander died young, at thirty-three; Caesar lived to the age of fifty-six. Alexander died of sickness, whereas Caesar was murdered. Alexander was born an absolute monarch; Caesar operated within the framework of a republic. Caesar's farthest conquest was Great Britain and he could not hold that one; Alexander stood at the gateway to India.

Of course the two subjects of parallel lives must have some differences, otherwise no interesting comparisons can be made. Hence, the question really resolves itself into how much sameness and how much difference there ought to be between any two men in order to make them suitable for Plutarch's purposes.

In many of our readings there is a strain that de-nounces luxuries. This is so in Plato's The Re-public, *in Aristotle's* Nicomachean Ethics, *in the life of Lycurgus, and there are hints of it else-where. What is a luxury and what is bad about it?*

Americans in general pride themselves on their high stand-ard of living, and in fact consider that a policy which prefers butter to guns is not only pleasing, but also a sign of peaceful intentions. Yet are not such expressions as "high standard of living" really synonyms for luxury?

A definition of luxury might be "anything beyond what is absolutely essential for sustaining life." Such a definition would, of course, make luxuries out of most things. Yet to denounce as luxuries all material possessions beyond the simplest clothes and the most primitive food would seem to renounce progress and civilization. Consider books, for in-stance. Are good books necessities or luxuries? And if the latter, how can any philosopher, such as Plato, be opposed to luxuries?

At the same time, we all feel there is something right about the fear of luxuries, and the sense that they weaken man's moral fiber. But what is the right degree of simplicity or luxury? Is the kind of simplicity that Lycurgus advocated good, when it deliberately teaches children to steal?

The following questions are designed to help you test the thoroughness of your reading. Each question is to be answered by giving a page or pages of the reading assignment. Answers will be found on page 190 of this Reading Plan.

1 What were Lycurgus' reasons for having twenty-eight senators?

2 How many lots of land were there for Sparta and her citizens?

3 What does Plutarch consider to have been Lycurgus' most effective stroke against luxury?

4 How did the Spartans treat their helots (slaves)?

5 What were the regulations concerning the Vestal virgins of Rome?

6 What did it mean when the gates of the temple of Janus were closed?

7 Why did Alexander object to Aristotle's publishing his works?

8 How did Diogenes react to Alexander's presence?

9   How did Clitus die?

10 Where was the decisive battle between Caesar and Pompey?

11 How did Caesar correct the calender?

12 On what occasion did Caesar refuse the crown of a Roman king?

OLD TESTAMENT

Book of Job

No matter how we define justice, we would all agree that to punish those who have done no wrong is unjust. We would also agree that it is unjust to reward those who have done nothing to deserve it or, worse, to reward those who, by their wrongdoing, deserve to be punished. Yet as we look around us we see men who *appear* to be righteous suffering all sorts of torment— the loss of their health, their worldly goods, their loved ones. In equally large numbers, we see men who *appear* to be vicious or corrupt enjoying the very things of which good men are deprived.

If this distribution of pleasures and pains represents the blind caprice of what Shakespeare calls "outrageous fortune," then, of course, what we have here is not a distribution of rewards and punishments by an all-seeing judge. What is entirely a matter of chance is neither just nor unjust. But if what befalls men represents the will of God, then we cannot help being sorely puzzled, especially if our belief in God is inseparable from our belief in the divine goodness and the justice which that entails.

Rather than accuse God of arrant injustice, we may question the appearances. Perhaps, the men who *seemed* to us to be good were, in God's eyes, *really* bad. But if the person who has suffered is ourselves and if, to the best of our knowledge, we are blameless, then we cry out, "Why?" That cry is Job's, and it has an answering echo in the heart of every man. Is the answer to the question to be found there also; or, if not, can we find it in the Book of Job?

Seventh Reading

I

The Book of Job is part of the so-called "wisdom literature" of the Jews. Other examples of this are such books of the Old Testament as Proverbs and Psalms. These works do not record Jewish history, nor do they embody the Mosaic law, nor are they prophetic in character. Instead they contain sayings of the sort that the wise and respected elders of a people might be expected to utter, or legends they might be expected to recount. The Book of Job dates from the post-Exilic period of the Jews; probably it was written near the end of the fifth century B.C.

II

The several parts of the Book of Job are easily distinguished. The first two chapters constitute an introduction, setting the stage; the last verses, i.e., 42:7–17; (D) 42:7–16, state the conclusion. The introduction and conclusion are written in prose, but the main portion of the book, 3:1 to 42:7, is cast in verse.

The narrative itself falls into several distinct parts. It begins with Job's complaint in Chapter 3, where Job "cursed his day." This is followed by three successive rounds of arguments between Job and his friends. The table on the following page summarizes the motion of the discussion.

This is followed by the long harangue of Elihu, in Chapters 32 to 37. It is thought that this is probably a later addition to the book.

God speaks to Job in Chapters 38–41, and Job submits himself to God at the end of the poem, 42:1–6.

In addition to the Elihu section, there are no doubt other

	First round	Second round	Third round
Eliphaz	Chap. 4–5	Chap. 15	Chap. 22
Job	Chap. 6–7	Chap. 16–17	Chap. 23–24
Bildad	Chap. 8	Chap. 18	Chap. 25
Job	Chap. 9–10	Chap. 19	Chap. 26–31
Zophar	Chap. 11	Chap. 20	———
Job	Chap. 12–14	Chap. 21	———

additions and interpolations; for instance, it is easy to see that Chapter 28, in praise of wisdom, is complete in itself and hardly belongs in the poem at all.

III

The problem with which Job wrestles may be indicated by a very simple question: How are divine rewards and punishments allocated? Or, more agonizingly: why, in God's universe, do the good sometimes suffer and the wicked prosper? We can see that this is a problem deeply embedded in the concepts of Judaeo-Christian religion by considering under what circumstances it would *not* be a problem.

First of all, it is clear that if there is no deity at all, then human happiness and prosperity cannot be interpreted as rewards given by God, nor can misfortunes be considered as divine punishments. Man's condition, in that case, must result from other causes.

Secondly, there is no problem about the distribution of divine rewards and punishments if, though God exists, he is considered as a capricious being, who acts according to no intelligible or rational rules at all. This is also another way of saying that, if God is not always and in all respects good, then he may well distribute his rewards and punishments not according to human merit, but capriciously or whimsically, like the Greek gods.

Closely related to this conception of God would be a view that denies God's omniscience, so that God might not know which men deserve rewards and which deserve punishments. Again, a God who cared nothing at all about men or a God who was actually evil could, of course, not be expected to distribute rewards and punishments to men on a just or rational basis.

Thirdly, if God is not all-powerful, then even though he wishes to reward the good and punish the bad, he may not always be able to execute his will. This would be the case if there are several equally powerful, or nearly equally powerful deities who compete with each other. For instance, in the *Odyssey* (see Vol. 4), several gods are in conflict over Odysseus' fate. While some favor and reward him, others send him misfortunes.

We can see, therefore, that on the positive side the problem of divine rewards and punishments arises from the conception of one God, a God who is good, omniscient, omnipotent, and governs the universe. For such a God—and this is the God of the Old and New Testaments—would be expected to reward the good and to punish the evil. Yet the daily experience of men shows that here on earth the opposite often appears to be the case.

This is the problem of the Book of Job; but it becomes even more complicated because the problem of divine justice must be viewed from two different perspectives.

On the one hand, there is the view from inside the poem— the problem as Job and his friends see it. This is what bothers them. Job was apparently a good and God-fearing man. He was prosperous and happy. For no apparent reason, he suddenly has been beset by all sorts of grave misfortunes. What is the explanation?

On the other hand, there is the view from outside the poem, i.e., the view which the reader gets who reads the introductory and concluding portions as well. This reader knows why Job suffers as he does; it is because God has permitted Satan to test Job's goodness and devotion to God. Satan claimed that Job's faithfulness was only skin-deep; if he were less prosperous, Satan claimed, Job would no longer obey and love God. Yet this explanation of Job's sufferings does not solve the problem of divine justice. For was it just of God to permit Job to be tested in this fashion? Does it not show a great unconcern for Job to expose him to the works of Satan? How can God be said to govern the universe if he permits Satan to do evil in it? Is the Book of Job, in other words, compatible with Genesis 1:31, where at the end of creation, it is said: "God saw everything that he had made, and, behold it was very good." Satan is certainly not *very good,* nor are the sufferings which he is permitted to inflict on Job *very good.*

IV

Job's three friends solve the problem in the most direct fashion. God punishes the wicked and only the wicked. Since God is punishing Job, Job must have been wicked. For instance, Eliphaz speaks to Job thus:

> Remember, I pray thee, who ever perished, being innocent? or where were the righteous cut off?
>
> Even as I have seen, they that plow iniquity, and sow wickedness, reap the same. (4:7–8)

And similarly, Bildad:

> Behold, God will not cast away a perfect man, neither will he help the evil doers. (8:20)

And finally, Zophar:

> Know therefore that God exacteth of thee less than thine iniquity deserveth. (11:6)

These quotations are all taken from the first round of arguments, but the friends continue in the same vein in the other two rounds.

Job denies their premise—that only the wicked are punished —by showing that many of the wicked prosper. Yet this is not surprising, he says, for they prosper only in order to be cut down eventually by God. So he denies that his misfortunes. prove him to be wicked, and in fact he maintains his own innocence. All of Chapter 31 is a long protestation of his own righteousness. "So these three men ceased to answer Job, because he was righteous in his own eyes." (32:1)

At this point Elihu appears on the scene; he is angry with both Job and his three friends:

> Against Job was his wrath kindled, because he justified himself rather than God.
>
> Also against his three friends was his wrath kindled, because they had found no answer, and yet had condemned Job. (32:2–3)

Most of his speech, however, seems to be directed against Job, for maintaining that he, Job, *is* just, which in turn, seems to imply that God is *not* just.

At this point, God intervenes and speaks to Job directly. He makes two speeches. The tone for the first one is set at the very beginning, when God asks: "Where wast thou when I laid the foundations of the earth?" (38:4) God goes on to enumerate the wonders of creation and to ask Job if he can do likewise. In the second speech, God invites Job to show his power:

> Deck thyself now with majesty and excellency; and array thyself with glory and beauty.
>
> Cast abroad the rage of thy wrath: and behold every one that is proud, and abase him.
>
> Look on every one that is proud, and bring him low; and tread down the wicked in their place.
>
> Hide them in the dust together; and bind their faces in secret.
>
> Then will I also confess unto thee that thine own right hand can save thee. (40:10–14; (D) 40:5–9)

From this we must construct the answer to the problem. It must be an answer that answers both Job and the other persons in the poem, and also the reader of the Book of Job who is aware of the wager between God and Satan.

One thing we can note at once: although everyone in the poem reproves Job, including God himself, nevertheless in the conclusion we read as follows:

> The Lord said to Eliphaz the Temanite, My wrath is kindled against thee, and against thy two friends: for ye have not spoken of me the thing that is right, as my servant Job hath. (42:7)

But what has Job said? He said that he, Job, was just. This we know to be true, for we know that his punishment is not due to any transgression, but to God's wager. He has also said that God does not always punish the wicked; he often lets them prosper, but in the end he will cast them down.

But this still leaves both Job and us, the readers, with the problem of God's justice. Why does God sometimes delay the punishment of the wicked? Why does God sometimes bring misery to the just? Why does God engage in a wager with Satan?

If Job has spoken rightly, there is only one part of his last speech that can give us a hint:

> I uttered that I understood not; things too wonderful for me, which I knew not. (42:3)

This confession of Job's and man's ignorance, of his inability to understand God's ways comes, of course, after God's speeches pointing to the many things that God can do and man cannot. They set the stage for this final admission of one more thing that God can do and man cannot: *Govern the world.*

V

This final admission of bafflement concerning God's decrees may remind us of a similar lack of understanding concerning the decrees of fate, which baffle the heroes of Greek tragedy. Nor is this the only similarity between the Book of Job and, say, *Oedipus the King.* In both, there is a hero, whether Oedipus or Job, who is afflicted with pride toward the divine powers. In both, there is a chorus, whether of Theban elders or of the three friends, which argues with the hero and points out to him his passion and his pride. In both the hero is a man of considerable stature and fortune, who is brought very low. We have already noted that the Book of Job was probably written around 400 B.C; in this external circumstance too, *Oedipus the King* and the Book of Job agree.

It is important, however, also to note the differences. The most important one is in the ending. Whereas Greek tragedy always ends with the hero ruined, Job recovers from his misfortunes and enjoys greater happiness than ever. Also lacking in the Book of Job is the notion that Job's pride was in any sense responsible for his misfortunes. And, of course, it must not be forgotten that the Book of Job was not written for the stage. The interested reader will find many other similarities and differences between the Book of Job and *Oedipus the King*.

VI

The preceding discussion has no doubt made it clear that there are many questions concerning the Book of Job that still remain to be answered. We shall proceed to consider some of them.

Is divine justice the same as human justice?

The answer here seems to be at once, no. For all the considerations of human justice indicate that a good man, such as Job, should not be made to suffer as Job did. But then, of course, the question arises whether Job was just in the divine eyes. Even assuming that he met all standards of human justice, is it not possible that he was still not just by the standards of divine justice?

In fact, is it not an integral part of Christian thought that no man is just, that we are all sinners only justified in the sight of God with the help of Christ? Again, this can be put in other terms: because of the stain of original sin, all mankind is sinful, in the Christian view, and hence no man, not even Job, *deserves* salvation and happiness. Thus the Book of Job may be a kind of bridge between the Old and the New Testaments.

Are God's rewards and punishments given in this life or in the next?

The three friends of Job clearly think that God's justice is fulfilled in this life and on that basis they find Job sinful. But if this is not so, if God rewards and punishes men in the next life, then the ups and downs of *this* life are morally insignificant. The New Testament is explicit in saying that men must look to the next life for their rewards and punishments; the Old Testament however is not so completely clear on this point.

Did Job obtain what was due him?

Were happiness, prosperity, and good fortune due to Job? Are they the due of every man who is just and good?

Here we must wonder what the meaning of the word "due" is. Does Job's justice *compel* God to be good to him? Can any man compel God to do anything or *deserve* anything of God? Is not the denial of this the point of the challenge that God hurls at Job, when he urges Job to show his power (see 40: 6–14; (D) 40:1–9).

Does the word "due" mean, perhaps, that happiness must necessarily come to Job? Such a presumption is mere folly; the Greek tragedians also knew that present happiness is no guarantee of continued good fortune; and here again we come back to the Aristotelian (and Platonic) distinction between happiness and good fortune.

How are God's actions compatible with his goodness?

It may be that no man can be sufficiently good to deserve anything except punishment. But would it not be a surer sign of divine goodness—if not justice—if God were to reward men like Job, who are as just as it is possible for men to be, rather than those who are clearly wicked?

This is one of the shoals on which thought about God and his goodness always threatens to founder. Job did not solve the problem intellectually. Instead, when God speaks to him directly and shows him his own weakness and ignorance, he submits—without understanding—to God's will (see 42:3).

God's providence, of course, extends beyond Job and his concerns. It takes in also his three friends; also Elihu; also Satan. Could it be argued that, at the price of the evil suffered by Job, good is brought into the world? That good might be the increased knowledge and humility of Eliphaz, Bildad, Zophar, Elihu, and Job himself; and also the humiliation of Satan.

Is Job adequately rewarded for his steadfastness? Are his sufferings made good?

It is noted early in the book that Job lost his seven sons and three daughters. At the end, he has seven more sons and three new daughters. Is this a fair exchange? In strictly human terms this substitution would leave something to be desired as an adequate reward or compensation; not only do the ten lost children appear to be forgotten, but it seems unlikely that any father (again, *in strictly human terms*) would be so easily satisfied. Still we must consider Abraham's willingness to sacrifice Isaac, and God's sacrifice of *his* Son.

The following questions are designed to help you test the thoroughness of your reading. Each question is to be answered by giving a page or pages of the reading assignment. Answers will be found on page 190 of this Reading Plan.

1 How many wagers does Satan make with God?

2 Is Job's wife as steadfast as he?

3 What are Job's arguments for suicide?

4 What is the difference, according to Job, between a tree that has been cut down and a dead man?

5 What is wisdom?

6 What are the final words of Job?

ST. AUGUSTINE

The Confessions

Books I–VIII

Vol. 18, pp. 1–61

Of all relationships, that between a man and the God he loves is perhaps the most intimate. The prayers such a man utters inwardly, the confession of his weakness and his need for help, the adoration and the worship with which he lifts his eyes up to the Almighty, are such private matters that no one but God can be privy to them. They are secrets from everyone else simply because they are incommunicable to other men. Even were we to overhear their verbal articulation, we would be hearing words only, words that could not have the same personal meaning for us.

Why, then, did St. Augustine put into a book feelings and thoughts which are addressed to God? God knows them before they were set forth in writing and, after the book is written, we who read it remain outsiders—like readers of a love letter. Yet there is good reason to believe that St. Augustine intended it for us to read. Instead of asking why he wrote it, the question to ask, perhaps, is what he hoped we might learn from reading it.

The writer of an autobiography usually regards his life as of sufficient interest to justify other men in learning about it. But while we can learn something about the growth of St. Augustine's mind and the development of his character by reading *The Confessions*, that would not seem to be his reason for publishing the book. Can it be that he hopes us to learn something about ourselves—the secret about ourselves which only God knows and we can learn only by examining ourselves as St. Augustine did?

Eighth Reading

I

Although Augustine calls this book his confessions, a perusal of only a few pages will suffice to convince you that, as Augustine uses the word, it carries no special emphasis on revelations of interesting misconduct. Augustine *does* discuss his misconduct; but he is much less worried about his apparently quite considerable record as a libertine than he is about events which may seem much more innocent to us, such as his childhood theft of some worthless pears.

Any writer of biography or of autobiography reserves for himself the right to be selective, to emphasize certain incidents and to omit others, for the sake of his purpose. We need only look back to Plutarch's *Lives* to find this confirmed. Augustine obviously makes use of the privilege; he by no means gives us a full factual account of the events of his life, and the events he does mention are often outwardly insignificant.

A great many things are omitted from the story of his life; indeed, many years seem to be completely forgotten. And many things are added that need not be present in an autobiography. For *The Confessions* is not simply an autobiography. Not only are the facts chosen in such a way as to serve Augustine's purpose—clearly the praise of God—but the facts are also interpreted in such a way that they seem to declare the glory of God, where another writer might interpret them altogether differently.

An example of this sort of thing occurs in Book I, when Augustine describes his boyhood studies and notes how he loved to read Latin, especially Virgil, but how he hated the study of Greek (p. 5d ff.). He is not content simply to remark that the study of reading and writing is more important, in his opinion, than the study of poetry. He calls on God to certify this: "But now, my God, cry Thou aloud in my soul, and let Thy truth tell me, 'Not so, not so. Far better was that first study.'" (p. 6b) Everything that Augustine reports is, in a word, related to God. *The Confessions* has aptly been called a prayer.

II

What is the book about? That question is not difficult to answer, especially in the light of what we have just said. Its overriding theme is clearly man's relation to God; and this is exemplified in terms of one man's relation to God, i.e., Augustine's.

This relationship, in Augustine's case, goes through all sorts of stages, climaxed by his conversion. But although it takes a long time to reach the actual conversion, Augustine is throughout in *some* relation to God, either fearing him, doubting him, misunderstanding him, seeking him, rejecting him, or, finally, accepting him. We shall examine some of the major ups and downs in Augustine's religious life.

There is one event in Book I which is, in a way, typical of the rest of the book. It occurs in Sections 17–18 (p. 5b–d). Augustine fell seriously ill; his mother, who was already a Christian, wanted to have him baptized. Since, however, Augustine suddenly recovered, the baptism was deferred. We know, of course, that the rest of *The Confessions* is nothing but a continuation of this story: baptism tentatively resolved on and yet postponed again and again. Very appropriately for the whole book, Augustine asks:

> I beseech Thee, my God, I would fain know, if so Thou willest, for what purpose my baptism was then deferred? (p. 5c)

The answer seems to be that it was done in order that he might be able to sin with greater impunity, since he was believed not yet ready for baptism. He wonders about the cogency of that reasoning:

But as to bodily health, no one says, "Let him be worse wounded, for he is not yet healed." (p. 5c)

But if this deferment of baptism was due to Augustine's mother, later postponements are his own doing; and the reason is exactly the one he deplores in the first book. He keeps postponing baptism because he does not feel ready to give up his sins. Thus in Book VIII, addressing God, he says:

When Thou didst on all sides shew me that what Thou saidst was true, I, convicted by the truth, had nothing at all to answer, but only those dull and drowsy words, "Anon, anon," "presently," "leave me but a little." (p. 56b)

And a little later:

But I wretched, most wretched, in the very commencement of my early youth, had begged chastity of Thee, and said, "Give me chastity and continency, only not yet." For I feared lest Thou shouldest hear me soon, and soon cure me of the disease of concupiscence, which I wished to have satisfied, rather than extinguished. (p. 57d)

Certainly, then, one of the main themes of *The Confessions* is sin, and man's—or Augustine's—inability to overcome it, even when he recognizes it as sin.

III

But Augustine's struggle is not only against the strength of his passions. He also has genuine intellectual doubts that need to be overcome before he can become a Christian.

His first doubt is more a matter of pride than anything else. In his initial look at the Scriptures they seem to him to say lowly and simple things and not, for instance, to be comparable in their tone and manner with the writings of Cicero (see Book III, 9, p. 15a–b).

Much more serious and disturbing to him are his later doubts, which led him toward a materialistic conception of God and toward Manicheanism.

Manicheanism is a theory that is distinguished principally by its clear dualism. It maintains that there are in the world two equal principles, one of good or light, and one of evil or darkness. These two struggle with each other; sometimes the one is in ascendance, and sometimes the other. The evil in the world consequently is due to the evil principle—when it prevails, evil comes into the world.

This theory has certain advantages over orthodox Christianity in explaining the facts of the world. Though Manicheanism was a separate religion (its originator, Mani, lived for the most part in Persia), it can be adapted to Christianity by interpreting God as the principle of goodness, and Satan as the principle of evil. It then becomes easy to reconcile the existence of evil in the world with the goodness of God: evil is simply due to the work of the devil.

In Book V, 20, Augustine tells us how he conceived God in this Manichean and materialistic fashion:

> And because a piety, such as it was, constrained me to believe, that the good God never created any evil nature, I conceived two masses, contrary to one another, both unbounded, but the evil narrower, the good more expansive. . . . And I seemed to myself more reverential, if I believed of Thee, my God . . . as unbounded, at least on other sides, although on that one where the mass of evil was opposed to Thee, I was constrained to confess Thee bounded; than if on all sides I should imagine Thee to be bounded by the form of the human body. And it seemed to me better to believe Thee to have created no evil (which to me ignorant seemed . . . a bodily substance, because I could not conceive of mind unless as a subtile body, and that diffused in definite spaces) than to believe the nature of evil, such as I conceived it, could come from Thee. (pp. 32d–33a)

The problem with which Augustine here struggles is, of course, the very problem we encountered when trying to interpret the Book of Job. How is it that there is evil in the world, when God is good? The Manichean answer is that although God is good, he is not all-powerful and that evil is a co-equal principle in the world.

In the Book of Job, it is clear that Satan is not an evil power equal to God. Satan is there quite clearly inferior to God and, in fact, can do his mischief only because God permits him to do so. Satan, in other words, is in the service of God. The view in the Book of Job, then, upholds God's omnipotence; but it may appear to leave the cause of evil still to be explained.

Augustine's answer to the problem is found in Book VII. In Book VII, 5, he begins to consider the notion that "free-will was the cause of our doing ill." But at first he finds this notion unsatisfactory. For man is made by God; and if man does evil through willing evil, is not God responsible for this evil? For why did God make man of such an evil nature that man wills evil?

In Book VII, 18, Augustine corrects this error, when he recognizes that evil is not something, i.e., it is not a substance. There is no thing, in other words, which can be pointed at and about which it can be said: It is evil.

> That evil then, which I sought whence it is, is not any substance: for were it a substance, it should be good. For either it should be an incorruptible substance, and so a chief good; or a corruptible substance, which, unless it were good, could not be corrupted. I perceived therefore, and it was manifested to me, that Thou madest all things good, nor is there any substance at all which Thou madest not. . . . (p. 49b)

Thus man cannot blame God for having created him evil. For man and everything else that God created are good insofar as they are. Evil comes into the world from free will which turns to something that is less good in preference to a greater good.

> And I enquired what iniquity was, and found it to be no substance, but the perversion of the will, turned aside from Thee, O God, the Supreme, towards these lower things. . . . (Book VII, 22, p. 50a–b)

On such a theory there obviously is no absolute evil, no principle to compete with God. There are only greater and lesser goods. Evil consists not in choosing something intrinsically evil, but in choosing a lesser good rather than a greater one.

An immediate example of this is provided by Augustine's own life: he refuses to be baptized, because he prefers the pleasures of the flesh. Now these pleasures, having been instituted by God, are also good; but to prefer them to the good of loving God is, of course, in the Christian view, evil. Augustine himself remarks on this, when he recalls his final moments of indecision just before his baptism (see Book VIII, 22–24).

IV

Several questions naturally come to mind in the course of this story of conversion. We shall try to discuss a few of them.

To whom is the book addressed? For whom is it written?

The first part of the question answers itself; the book is addressed to God, as we can see by looking at the first chapter and noting that Augustine repeatedly calls on God.

But this immediately leads us to the second part of the question. Why is the book addressed to God? Is it written for God? It certainly cannot be written "for God" in the sense of intending to benefit God; nothing that a man can do can benefit God.

And related to this is also the query: Why is the book written? Two persons are most intimately concerned with the events of the book; namely, God and Augustine. But these two persons are also the two that least need to be told what happened, for both know it exactly. Augustine knows what happened because it happened to him; God knows it, because he knows everything.

Nevertheless, we can perhaps derive the rudiments of an answer from all these negative points. Since the book is not meant to benefit God, it is probably meant to benefit Augustine. Its purpose is not to tell anything new to either God or the writer. It would seem to be written "for God" as something given to him by Augustine. It is an offering from Augustine of the best thing he has to give; but this best thing, his conversion, is itself something that has come from God.

Who converts Augustine?

The meaning of this question becomes clearer if we ask, Does Augustine convert himself? And then either an affirmative or a negative answer presents us with puzzles. The affirmative answer, first of all, does not seem to be true. Augustine's conversion is delayed again and again; and what makes it finally happen are the events in the garden—the voice calling on Augustine to read, and his reading a particular passage from Scripture. All this seems to be caused by God. Furthermore, the notion of man by his own power reaching God goes contrary to the teachings of Christianity. For instance, original sin is thought to have wounded human nature so that man is no longer able to do good by himself. Least of all can he achieve by himself his supreme good, i.e., union with God.

But if we take the negative answer, it, too, has its difficulties. For if Augustine did not convert himself, then it must have been God who accomplished this. In that case, no merit attaches to Augustine for his conversion. On the other hand, we must also wonder, if all this was God's doing, why did God delay so long—why were there all the hesitations, false starts, and torments of Augustine?

It would seem that an acceptable solution must somehow steer a middle course between the affirmative and negative answers that we have outlined. Something must be contributed by Augustine to his own conversion, and yet the power to turn to God must also come from God.

Why did Augustine consider the pear theft so serious?

Was a really serious sin involved in this theft, or is Augustine simply being morally over-fastidious? Augustine himself considers the arguments that might be brought to lessen the offense: a small value was involved, boys will be boys, others have done the same thing, etc. His answer, of course, is that the theft of the pears was so serious, because he did not really desire the pears at all; rather, he stole for the sake of stealing. In more generalized terms, he sinned for the sake of sinning.

What would be a sin committed not for the sake of sinning? Suppose the theft had been committed in order to enjoy the flavor of the fruit, i.e., in order to eat it. Then the sin would consist in preferring a lesser good—the pleasure to be derived from eating the pear—to a greater good, viz., obeying God's commandment, *Thou shalt not steal.*

The question then is why such a sin is a lesser one than the sin which consists in preferring sinning to doing good. We can hardly help being reminded by this incident of a comparable theft—of an apple—at the beginning of the world. Does this passage indirectly throw light on the sin of Adam?

Do you agree with the contention that there is no principle of evil in the world, but only lesser goods?

The contention that there is no absolute evil amounts to saying that everything which is, is good. This is the same as Augustine's argument that evil cannot be a substance, for a substance is either incorruptible and so good, or if corruptible, then it is at least in part good so that it can be corrupted. Or in brief: everything which is, or every substance, is good; hence evil cannot be a substance.

But does it seem correct that everything is good? Can dirt, disease, poverty, pain, crime, brutality, be interpreted as merely lesser goods? In what sense is pain a good? In what sense is disease a good?

If everything that is, is good, how can there be degrees of goodness or degrees of badness? It would appear to involve the notion of degrees of being. Is there such a thing as a greater and lesser degree of being; i.e., *are* some things more perfect beings than others?

The following questions are designed to help you test the thoroughness of your reading. Each question is to be answered by giving a page or pages of the reading assignment. Answers will be found on page 190 of this Reading Plan.

1 What book turned Augustine to God when he was in Carthage?

2 Who was the Bishop of the Manichees that Augustine hoped would solve his doubts?

3 On the basis of what arguments did Augustine reject the validity of astrology?

4 What did the voice in the garden say to Augustine that caused his conversion?

5 What was the difference in students' behavior in Carthage and in Rome?

6 What was Alypius' attitude toward gladiatorial games?

7 What reason does Augustine give for reciting his sins?

8 What was the rule for the interpretation of Scriptures that Augustine learned from Ambrose?

MONTAIGNE

The Essays

T he two great maxims of human wisdom which
come down to us from antiquity are "Know thyself"
and "Nothing overmuch." Montaigne's essays represent a lifetime spent in the sustained effort to know
himself and to follow the counsel of moderation in
all things. Yet his self-examination stands in sharp
contrast to that of St. Augustine, for it is not directed
toward judging himself or toward mending his ways.
Nor does it appear to be motivated by the insight of
Socrates that "an unexamined life is not worth living."
Montaigne's interest seems simply to be that of an
explorer to whom nothing human is foreign or strange.
He carried on his explorations by reading the great

books, by listening to the opinions of other men, by observing the variety of customs and the conflict of beliefs.

Confronted by the welter of opinions, customs, and beliefs, among which he found none so universal as to lack a contrary, Montaigne adopted the policy of suspended judgment. This is the mark of his special brand of skepticism and tolerance. It challenges us as does the faith of St. Augustine and the devotion of Socrates to the pursuit of truth. In Montaigne's presence, as in theirs, we cannot close our minds to possibilities we have not explored; we cannot rest assured that we have found the answers; we cannot avoid questioning our inherited prejudices. If those prejudices are the ones most widely prevalent today, we may be initially more responsive to Montaigne, but he will expose us to their prodding as well as his own and, under their conjoint influence, we cannot help understanding ourselves a little better.

Ninth Reading

I

The essay is unlike any of the other forms of writing that we have come across so far. It may, in fact, be said to have been invented by Montaigne. What kind of writing is the essay? Why did Montaigne adopt this particular literary form?

He himself gives us some idea of what he is doing in his prefatory note to the reader (p. 1).

> Reader, thou hast here an honest book; it doth at the outset forewarn thee that, in contriving the same, I have proposed to myself no other than a domestic and private end: I have had no consideration at all either to thy service or to my glory. . . . I have dedicated it to the particular commodity of my kinsfolk and friends, so that, having lost me (which they must do shortly), they may therein recover some traits of my conditions and humours, and by that means preserve more whole, and more life-like, the knowledge they had of me. . . . Thus, reader, myself am the matter of my book. . . .

The great French writer here reveals what is perhaps the most outstanding property of his essays: their intensely personal character. In reading them, we are constantly conscious of the author. Not only are the essays written in the first person, but Montaigne makes constant reference to his personal experience, to his family, to his reading. And this is not accidental; for as he says in the prefatory remark, Montaigne is the matter of Montaigne's book.

We have come across another book in our reading that is intensely personal, namely, Augustine's *Confessions*. Yet the way in which these two books are personal and author-centered is quite different.

Neither work is actually very rich in biographical materials, although there are probably more facts about Montaigne scattered in *The Essays* than there are about Augustine in *The Confessions*. But, in reading Augustine, we are always conscious that this book is written for a purpose: as a work of moral instruction, of edification, of Christian apologetics.

In reading Montaigne, on the other hand, we are conscious that these essays are said, again and again, to be in the nature of leisurely speculation. Even granting that their very casualness is no doubt a sign of great art on Montaigne's part, it remains true that no single concern pulses through these essays. The most we can say is that as Augustine pointedly glorifies God, so Montaigne in passing depreciates man. It may be observed parenthetically that both men are preoccupied, in radically different ways, with the problem of good and evil.

But to say that the essays are the reflections of leisure hours is not to say that they are either without purpose or without value. They reflect Montaigne—not through his actions, nor the torments of his conscience, but through the musings of his mind. And in reflecting Montaigne, the essays also picture for us the culture of France and Europe in the sixteenth century.

It was, of course, a time of ferment and change. America had just been discovered; the Reformation was going on in Germany; the dawn of the "modern" era was less than 100 years away. Montaigne's *Essays,* insofar as they have one uniform characteristic, give evidence of this feeling of change and unsettledness: Nothing, Montaigne says over and over, can be taken for granted; what seems good to us seems evil to other people.

Montaigne's views no doubt influenced many, among them Shakespeare. Hamlet's remark that "nothing is either good or bad, but thinking makes it so" is almost a quotation of the title, "That the Relish of Good and Evil Depends in a Great Measure upon the Opinion We Have of Them." If we wanted to apply a label to Montaigne, we should have to call him a skeptic. Not that he is one in the extreme sense (which reduces its advocate to nothing but silence), but he does believe that no view is to be taken for granted simply because custom and received opinion favor it.

He can hardly be said to argue. He does not establish his position by demonstration or disputation. His chief tools of persuasion are, instead, the use of quotations (and these, as we have already noted, are often from Plutarch, although he also favors such Latin authors as Virgil, Ovid, and Livy) and the descriptions of the habits and customs of other peoples and nations. Thus he makes his points by the use of examples, rather than by strict reasoning.

Both in method and in intent, then, Montaigne is not a philosopher. Even when he urges upon us "That the relish of good and evil depends in a great measure upon the opinion we have of them," he is not being a moral philosopher. For he is not defending a theory of moral relativity; he is not maintaining that good and evil *are* merely what people think they are. Instead, he merely reports the fact of moral relativity. "The relish of good and evil," i.e., our enjoyment of something as good or bad, depends on our opinion of what is good or bad. Thus he exemplifies the fact—no doubt true—that in moral matters we are influenced greatly in our feelings by what we think we ought to feel. It is interesting to note that Shakespeare, in the words of Hamlet, makes a much stronger statement; i.e., that nothing *is* either good or bad apart from our opinion.

II

In aim and outlook, though not in method, Montaigne is akin to the modern social scientist. His concerns and subject matter fall into the fields of history, anthropology, psychology, and sociology; all of these are the branches of social or behavioral science. And so, though the matter of his book is in one way himself, in another it is all of human behavior.

In studying the customs and behavior of other peoples and other times Montaigne does not, of course, employ a method based on strict observation or experimentation. He does not undertake anthropological field trips nor report on those of others. Instead, the material on which he draws comes to him from writers, travelers, hearsay, and most often from sources that he does not identify at all.

In the essay, "Of Custom," there is a catalogue of various and strange customs that encompasses almost everything imaginable. Beginning on page 44c, and ending on page 46b, Montaigne recites different manners of dressing, of eating, of sexual behavior, of worshiping, of fighting, and so forth.

One subject which seems to fascinate him is that of cannibalism. In the catalogue just mentioned, he merely notes in passing (45d) that "in one place, men feed upon human flesh." But a little later, when he wants to illustrate how contrary behavior may be sanctioned in different countries by custom, he comes back to the subject.

> Darius asking certain Greeks what they would take to assume the custom of the Indians, of eating the dead bodies of their fathers (for that was their use, believing they could not give them a better, nor more noble sepulture, than to bury them in their own bodies), they made answer, that nothing in the world should hire them to do it; but having also tried to persuade the Indians to leave their custom, and, after the Greek manner, to burn the bodies of their fathers, they conceived a still greater horror at the notion. (pp. 46d–47a)

Finally, Montaigne returns to the subject in the essay entitled "Of Cannibals." Speaking of the inhabitants of newly discovered America, he says:

> I find that there is nothing barbarous or savage in this nation, by anything that I can gather, excepting, that every one gives the title of barbarism to everything that is not in use in his own country. . . . They are savages at the same rate that we say fruits are wild, which nature produces of herself and by her own ordinary progress; whereas in truth, we ought rather to call those wild, whose natures we have changed by our artifice, and diverted from the common order. (p. 93b–c)

And a little later he comments, surely not without justice, on cannibalism as compared to the religious strife brought on by the Reformation:

I conceive there is more barbarity in eating a man alive, than when he is dead; in tearing a body limb from limb by racks and torments, that is yet in perfect sense; in roasting it by degrees; in causing it to be bitten and worried by dogs and swine (as we have not only read, but lately seen, not amongst inveterate and mortal enemies, but among neighbours and fellow-citizens, and, which is worse, under colour of piety and religion), than to roast and eat him after he is dead. (p. 95c)

III

Are all customs equally good?

Consider the following remarks of Montaigne:

There is nothing, in my opinion, that [custom] does not, or may not do; and, therefore, with very good reason it is, that Pindar calls her the queen, and empress of the world. He that was seen to beat his father, and reproved for so doing, made answer, that it was the custom of their family: that, in like manner his father had beaten his grandfather, his grandfather his great-grandfather, "And this," says he, pointing to his son, "when he comes to my age, shall beat me." And the father, whom the son dragged and hauled along the streets, commanded him to stop at a certain door, for he himself, he said, had dragged his father no farther, that being the utmost limit of the hereditary outrage the sons used to practise upon the fathers in their family. (p. 46b)

If we take the quotation and the story it tells at face value, there is no doubt that it powerfully supports the contention that custom is a very strong force, whether in the life of individuals, families, or nations.

But does the quotation also support the view that all customs are equally good? It apparently does not; for Montaigne himself, in the last sentence uses the word "outrage" to describe a custom. Thus he envisages an event which, while sanctioned by custom, is still outrageous.

Perhaps, however, the analysis needs to be carried a little further. For the particular custom which Montaigne mentions and condemns is not a generally shared one; it is the custom of only one family. Here we may wonder, first of all, whether a family can have a "custom." It may be that that term ought to be restricted to usages more widely followed than by one family.

But even if we admit that something may be called customary although it applies to only a small group or even one person (for example, there is nothing unusual in a man saying, "I customarily drink coffee in the morning"), we can ask whether the number of people who follow a custom has a bearing on its goodness.

It may be that Montaigne would consider a custom followed by all or nearly all the people of a certain country or area to be automatically good. If that should turn out to be his position, it would still be possible to maintain that, of customs held by small groups, some are better than others. Indeed, since such customs will often conflict with one another, it cannot be said that all such customs are good. Thus it would be possible to say that one family's custom of sons beating their fathers is not good, because it conflicts with the more generally held custom of sons honoring their fathers.

Is custom itself responsible for what we consider good or bad?

We must try to relate the two essays involved, viz., "On Custom" and "The Relish of Good and Evil." The first one points out the power of custom; the second one maintains that good and evil are a matter of opinion. Now the question naturally suggests itself, what gives us the opinion concerning good and evil? It may be that custom is responsible even for this. In that case, what we think is good or evil depends on the customary judgments of good and evil that have been and are being made around us. If it is the custom of a certain people or group of people to condemn some kind of action as bad, then any member of that group will form his opinion of good and evil in accordance with that custom.

How does this position affect moral judgment? Can we say, for example, that a person who practices racial or religious discrimination in a society or area where such practice is customary is guilty of anything? Have we any ground, in this view, for condemning the Communist in a Communist country, the Nazi in a Nazi country, the head-hunter, the old Chinese who exposed their newborn daughters to death by the elements? We may try to make a moral distinction in all such matters, between "leaders" and "followers," but leaders, too, may be seen themselves to have been shaped by customary views of good and evil.

Does the view that custom determines the judgments of good and evil have any effect on the question whether a custom itself can be good or evil? At first glance, it may seem that the notion that custom determines which customs are good or bad is not defensible, but this need not be so. Certainly we can see that custom in the United States causes us to regard the custom of eating horse meat, practiced in some other countries, as bad or unpleasant. Or again, in the nineteenth century, the custom of our country as a whole played a large part in forming the judgment that the custom of polygamy, practiced by a religious minority, the Mormons, was deplorable.

What does seem to be the case is that if there is a custom practiced by all the members of a group, then there can hardly be a customary judgment within that group that the custom is bad. Any evaluation of the customs of a group apparently has to be based not on the customs of that group, but either on the customs of some other group or on a concept of good that is not derived from custom.

Do you agree with Montaigne's view that philosophy should be studied by the young?

Though Montaigne is an admirer of Socrates and of Plato, he apparently does not agree with the latter's opinion in *The Republic* that philosophy should be studied by the experienced and mature. Here is what Montaigne says:

> Since philosophy is that which instructs us to live, and that infancy has there its lessons as well as other ages, why is it not communicated to children betimes? . . .
> They begin to teach us to live when we have almost done living. A hundred students have got the pox before they have come to

read Aristotle's lecture on temperance. Cicero said, that though he should live two men's ages, he should never find leisure to study the lyric poets; and I find these sophisters yet more deplorably unprofitable. The boy we would breed has a great deal less time to spare; he owes but the first fifteen or sixteen years of his life to education; the remainder is due to action. Let us, therefore, employ that short time in necessary instruction. Away with the thorny subtleties of dialectics, they are abuses, things by which our lives can never be amended: take the plain philosophical discourses, learn how rightly to choose, and then rightly to apply them; they are more easy to be understood than one of Boccaccio's novels; a child from nurse is much more capable of them, than of learning to read or to write. Philosophy has discourses proper for childhood, as well as for the decrepit age of men. (p. 72b–c)

It is possible to find considerable fault with this passage. The following questions could all be put to Montaigne as the beginning of a critical examination of his meaning here. Is the purpose of philosophy really to instruct us how to live? Does philosophy not have at least other purposes as well? Is the purpose of philosophy primarily practical, i.e., directed toward teaching us what to do, how to live; or is its purpose primarily theoretic, i.e., directed toward the acquisition of knowledge?

Why should only fifteen or sixteen years be given over to education? Does it not make more sense to say that a man's education is never finished, except in the accidental sense of his having finished certain formal requirements? Is not moral philosophy fully understandable only to the person who has experienced the full range of moral dilemmas—that is, the adult?

What are the plain philosophical discourses that Montaigne recommends for study? They do not seem altogether plain, when he goes on to say that the boy should learn rightly to choose and then to apply them. That, after all, seems anything but plain. The whole difficulty of moral education is not to learn rules and maxims, but to know how to apply them.

How valid is Montaigne's argument that good and evil depend on opinion?

Near the beginning of his essay on the subject, Montaigne writes as follows:

> If the original being of those things we fear had power to lodge itself in us by its own authority, it would then lodge itself alike, and in like manner, in all; for men are all of the same kind, and saving in greater and less proportions, are all provided with the same utensils and instruments to conceive and to judge; but the diversity of opinions we have of those things clearly evidences that they only enter us by compositions; one person, peradventure, admits them in their true being, but a thousand others give them a new and contrary being in them. (p. 115c–d)

Now what does this argument prove? It purports to show (and we may grant it succeeds in showing) that how we think of something depends on us as well as on the thing we think about. We recall once more that the full title of the essay is "That the *relish* of good and evil depends in *a great measure* upon the opinion we have of them" (italics added). Two things, therefore, are *not* claimed by Montaigne: (1) that the relish of good and evil depends *entirely* on the opinion we have of them, or (2) that good and evil *themselves* depend on our opinion of them.

Does the essay title then say anything more than "That the opinion of good and evil depends in a great measure upon the opinion we have of them"? Perhaps it is not fair to equate "relish" with "opinion"; but in any case relish is something subjective, like taste. And that relish should therefore depend on opinion seems hardly very surprising.

The following questions are designed to help you test the thoroughness of your reading. Each question is to be answered by giving a page or pages of the reading assignment. Answers will be found on page 190 of this Reading Plan.

1 What does Montaigne make of the story that an ancient philosopher did not want to acknowledge pain as an evil?

2 Which does Montaigne think is more important in practical matters: learning or judgment?

3 What is the chief educational use of travel?

4 In Montaigne's view is philosophy a difficult and severe discipline?

5 How did Montaigne learn Latin?

6 What is Montaigne's opinion of novelty?

SHAKESPEARE

Hamlet

Vol. 27, pp. 29–72

Of all works of dramatic poetry, perhaps even of all works of Western literature, *Hamlet* is probably the best-known book, just as Shakespeare is probably the best-known author. Everyone knows something about the character of Hamlet and something of his trials and tribulations; and most people have either read the play or seen it produced on the stage or on the screen. Far from detracting from a careful reading or re-reading of the play, that makes it all the more exciting. Anyone who thinks he knows the story, or that he has figured Hamlet out, is in for a big surprise. The more one examines the play, the more one finds in the intricacy of its plot and the complexity of its leading character. Like a living person, *Hamlet* becomes more interesting and more puzzling with growing intimacy.

Our familiarity with *Hamlet* is not just a matter of our acquaintance with the man or the story. The language of the play is so much in our everyday speech that reading it is like reading a book of quotations.

Here is a small sampling of the phrases or sentences that, as we read them, we remember having heard before or even having spoken: "Frailty, thy name is woman"; "Neither a borrower nor a lender be"; "Give every man thy ear, but few thy voice"; "This above all: to thine own self be true"; "Giving more light than heat"; "To the manner born"; "It is a custom more honour'd in the breach than the observance"; "Something is rotten in the state of Denmark"; "Leave her to heaven"; "The time is out of joint"; "Brevity is the soul of wit"; "Though this be madness, yet there is method in't"; "There is nothing either good or bad, but thinking makes it so"; "Conscience does make cowards of us all"; "To be, or not to be: that is the question"; "Ay, there's the rub"; "Suit the action to the word"; "Sweets to the sweet"; "The rest is silence."

The magic of this play cannot be better demonstrated than by the extent to which its language, its problems, and its wisdom have become everyone's property. To become better acquainted with it through another, carefully guided, reading is to become more intensely alive, not only to oneself but to the civilization of which we are a part.

Tenth Reading

I

It may be interesting to compare Hamlet with the Sophoclean tragedies of the third reading assignment. The differences and similarities are subtle, perhaps, but consideration of the idea of tragedy itself may throw some light on them. Aristotle, basing his view largely on *Oedipus the King*, gives the following definition of tragedy:

> A tragedy, then, is the imitation of an action that is serious and also, as having magnitude, complete in itself; in language with pleasurable accessories, each kind brought in separately in the parts of the work; in a dramatic, not in a narrative form; with in cidents arousing pity and fear, wherewith to accomplish its catharsis of such emotions. (*On Poetics*, Vol. 9, Ch. 6, p. 684a)

Chaucer has this to say about tragedy, at the end of his story about Croesus, in "The Monk's Tale":

> So hanged was Croesus, that proud Lydian king,
> His royal throne could nothing then avail.
> Tragedy is no other kind of thing;
> Nor can the singer cry aught, or bewail,
> But that Dame Fortune always will assail
> With unwarned stroke those great ones who are proud;
> For when men trust her most, then will she fail
> And cover her bright face as with a cloud.
> (*Canterbury Tales*, Vol. 22, pp. 446–447)

Your own reading of the plays, in the light of Aristotle and Chaucer, will suggest some of the similarities between Greek and Shakespearean tragedy. But it may be worth while to dwell a little on the differences, using *Hamlet* and *Oedipus the King* as the primary means of comparison.

There are certain obvious external differences. Shakespearean drama does not observe the classic unities of time, space, and action. While the Greek tragedy takes place in one location, in one short period of time, and concerns only one connected series of events, the Shakespearean often covers several years' time, moves across many miles, and employs several different, though related strands of actions. Thus in *Hamlet*, several weeks at least are taken up with Hamlet's travels to England, his capture by pirates, and his return; and similarly, the location of the play shifts from the tower of the castle, to rooms inside, to the churchyard, and other places.

Another easily apparent difference is the presence of the chorus in the Greek plays and its absence in Shakespeare. The role of the chorus suggests other, and perhaps more important, differences. Fate, fortune, and divine rule play a much more important part in *Oedipus the King* than in *Hamlet*. In the latter, human deliberation, motivation, and indecision are emphasized, while in the former we get more of a feeling of inescapable doom, to which every step of the hero brings him closer. Connected with the difference, no doubt, is the fact that Shakespearean tragedy almost always has some comic relief (such as the grave-diggers in Act V of *Hamlet*). Such a mixture of the comic and tragic is unthinkable for the Greek tragedian.

II

Hamlet is a bloody and, in many respects, a sensational play. By the end of the tragedy, eight of its characters (Claudius, Gertrude, Hamlet, Ophelia, Polonius, Laertes, Rosencrantz, Guildenstern) are dead. Interspersed in the play are such spectacular phenomena as a ghost, a play within the play, real and feigned madness, a fight within a freshly-dug grave, a rapier match.

What is it that brings about all these deaths and all this action? A brief review of the plot suffices to raise several questions about the play.

One might be tempted to summarize the play as follows: Hamlet, when he learns that his royal father has been killed by the present king, determines on revenge. But he hesitates

to execute his purpose. The play is taken up with his hesitations. Only in the last scene of the last act does the king meet
his deserved punishment.

It is obvious that there are several things wrong with this
summary. First, it omits the important fact that Claudius, the
present king, is the dead king's brother (and therefore Hamlet's
uncle), and that Claudius has not only killed his brother but
has compounded this offense by marrying his brother's widow,
Hamlet's mother.

Secondly, much more takes place in the body of the play
than Hamlet's hesitation (although that hesitation is usually
emphasized in popular theories about the play).

Thirdly, the death of Claudius is only one of eight deaths;
and four of these take place in the last scene. Furthermore, it
can hardly be said that Hamlet is merely meting out punishment to Claudius for killing the elder Hamlet. The queen is
already dead. Laertes and Hamlet are both mortally wounded
when Hamlet stabs Claudius. And he seems to kill the king
more for the treachery committed against himself (in having
Laertes use a poisoned sword), than for his earlier crimes.
"The King, the King's to blame," says Laertes, and Hamlet
replies,

> The point envenom'd too!
> Then, venom, to thy work.

It is then that he stabs the King.

But these are only the most obvious difficulties that the
play presents, if we wish to develop a consistent and plausible
theory of what happens and why it happens. Let us consider
some of the other puzzles that Shakespeare chose to put into
the play.

The first time that Hamlet appears, and before he has
spoken to his father's ghost (and before he knows, therefore,
that Claudius has murdered his father), he is described as dis-
tracted and cloudy in mien. The first time that he is alone (still
before he has seen the ghost), he reveals his mood:

> O, that this too too solid flesh would melt,
> Thaw, and resolve itself into a dew!
> Or that the Everlasting had not fix'd
> His canon 'gainst self-slaughter! O God! God!
> How weary, stale, flat, and unprofitable,
> Seem to me all the uses of this world!
> (Act I, Scene II, p. 32d)

In the rest of the soliloquy he indicates what makes him think of suicide even at this early stage of the play: it is his mother's quickness in contracting marriage after her first husband's death, a marriage, furthermore, that Hamlet considers incestuous. Yet nothing, he tells us, can be said about this, let alone be done about it (though he gives us no reason why not), and so he ends the speech with the line,

> But break, my heart; for I must hold my tongue.

In the fifth scene of the first act, Hamlet does see the ghost of his father and learns that he must not only accuse his mother of precipitate and incestuous marriage but also his uncle of the fratricide. The vision moves him to that anguished outcry:

> The time is out of joint: O cursed spite,
> That ever I was born to set it right!
> (Act I, Scene V, p. 39a)

But though he feels he must set things right, he does nothing. And so we find that in the last scene of Act II, after the players have been presented to Hamlet, he still has done nothing; nor does he have any plans. He reproaches himself for this strange inertness:

> O, what a rogue and peasant slave am I!
> . . . . This is most brave,
> That I, the son of a dear father murder'd,
> Prompted to my revenge by heaven and hell,
> Must, like a whore, unpack my heart with words,
> And fall a-cursing, like a very drab,
> A scullion!   (p. 46b–d)

But his reproaches do not result in his rushing upon the king;

he decides he must test whether the ghost was sent from heaven or hell, and so devises the play-within-the-play, wherein his father's murder is to be re-enacted before Claudius' eyes.

Before this test can take place, Hamlet's thoughts turn once more to suicide in the most famous soliloquy of the play:

> To be, or not to be: that is the question.
> Whether 'tis nobler in the mind to suffer
> The slings and arrows of outrageous fortune,
> Or to take arms against a sea of troubles,
> And by opposing end them? To die; to sleep;
> No more; and by a sleep to say we end
> The heart-ache and the thousand natural shocks
> That flesh is heir to, 'tis a consummation
> Devoutly to be wish'd. To die, to sleep;
> To sleep? perchance to dream. Ay, there's the rub;
> For in that sleep of death what dreams may come
> When we have shuffled off this mortal coil,
> Must give us pause. There's the respect
> That makes calamity of so long life. . . .
> Thus conscience does make cowards of us all;
> And thus the native hue of resolution
> Is sicklied o'er with the pale case of thought,
> And enterprises of great pitch and moment
> With this regard their currents turn awry,
> And lose the name of action.
> (Act III, Scene I, p. 47c–d)

If death were really the end, it would, perhaps, be desirable and men in torment would not hesitate at suicide. This is what Hamlet says; but it is interesting to recall what Socrates said about death in the *Apology:*

> Now if you suppose that [in death] there is no consciousness, but a sleep like the sleep of him who is undisturbed even by dreams, death will be an unspeakable gain. For if a person were to select the night in which his sleep was undisturbed even by dreams, and were to compare with this the other days and nights of his life, and then were to tell us how many days and nights he had passed in the course of his life better and more pleasantly than this one, I think that any man, I will not say a private man, but even the great king will not find many such days or nights, when compared with the others. Now if death be of such a nature, I say that to

die is gain; for eternity is then only a single night. (Vol. 7, p. 211b–c)

Neither Socrates nor Hamlet is sure that death is nothing but a dreamless sleep; but they agree that if it were, it would be no evil to man.

Now let us return to *Hamlet* and the play-within-the-play that is to test the ghost's veracity. The test accomplishes its purpose—the king, frightened, leaves the room in the middle of the performance. He retires to pray, and Hamlet comes upon Claudius while he is praying. Hamlet recognizes his chance:

Now might I do it pat, now he is praying;

but he decides against it, since to kill his uncle while he is praying would be to send him to heaven.

No!
Up, sword; and know thou a more horrid hent.
When he is drunk asleep, or in his rage,
Or in the incestuous pleasure of his bed;
At gaming, swearing, or about some act
That has no relish of salvation in't;
Then trip him, that his heels may kick at heaven,
And that his soul may be as damn'd and black
As hell, whereto it goes.
(Act III, Scene III, p. 54a–b)

However, in the very next scene, we see this hesitating Hamlet capable of the most precipitate action. He slays Polonius who is hiding behind a curtain in the queen's bedroom, while she and Hamlet are talking. Hamlet thinks it is the king he has killed, but when it turns out to be Polonius, his resolution seems again to fail, and he makes no protest about being sent to England. And it is not until he returns from England that the tragedy comes to its end.

III

The puzzle of the play is the character of Hamlet. Almost anything that we might be tempted to say concerning him can as easily be denied as affirmed. We can show this by considering a number of questions, and indicating the possible opposed answers.

Is Hamlet markedly hesitating and indecisive?

We have already indicated some of the evidence for an affirmative answer here. It consists, in summary, of such items as the following: (1) the fact that Hamlet's revenge is delayed to the very end of the play; (2) his self-accusations and doubts ("O, that this too too solid flesh would melt," *and* "O, what a rogue and peasant slave am I!" *and* "To be, or not to be: that is the question.") as expressed in the great soliloquies; (3) the fact that a decisive character would hardly talk to himself so much; (4) his inability to believe the ghost and his need to test its words; (5) his refusal to kill Claudius when he has the opportunity.

Is Hamlet decisive and resolute?

It may seem at first hard to bring support for an affirmative answer to this question. But it can be done. We recall things of the following sort: (1) Hamlet deals quickly and unhesitatingly with the ghost; (2) as soon as he hears that the players are visiting the castle, he decides to put them to his use and deals with them efficiently; (3) he stabs Polonius through the curtain, in an act that deserves more to be called rash than anything else; (4) he coolly turns Rosencrantz's and Guildenstern's treachery against themselves; (5) his behavior at Ophelia's grave and in the duel is that of a man held back by no doubts.

Finally, we may add that even when Hamlet decides against action, such decision itself constitutes action. Only if we have already decided that Hamlet must act in a certain way, can we interpret his contrary action—or inaction—as that of an ambivalent or compulsive personality.

Is Hamlet gentle and kind?

The over-all impression we get of Hamlet is certainly that he is kind and considerate. It is not always easy to support this impression, but there are nevertheless several events we can point to. In the same scene in which he accuses his mother and slays Polonius, he also treats Gertrude with kindness and love; his affection for Horatio throughout is unmistakable; the "alas, poor Yorick" speech shows definite signs of human compassion and understanding.

Is Hamlet gross and cruel?

Unfortunately, we can also support an affirmative answer to this question. The treatment which Ophelia receives at the hands of Hamlet in Act III, Scene I (the nunnery scene) is certainly cruel; and in Act III, Scene IV, Hamlet deals most severely with his mother. In fact, only the reappearance of his father's ghost seems to bring Hamlet to his senses.

Is Hamlet trusting and open?

In many respects he seems to be so. For instance, he never suspects that his father has been murdered until the ghost tells him. He does not suspect the plot to have him killed in England. Again, he is most trusting in accepting the foil given to him at the duel.

Is Hamlet crafty?

Here again we can summon affirmative evidence. The way in which he manages to dispatch Rosencrantz and Guildenstern is certainly indicative of a shrewd mind. Furthermore, the whole arrangement of the play-within-the-play in order to trap the king ("The play's the thing / Wherein I'll catch the conscience of the King") is clever and crafty.

Does the tragedy depend upon accidental factors?

In a way, it is the death of Polonius that leads to all the other deaths. Because he killed Polonius, Hamlet is sent to England and on the trip discovers the treachery of his uncle. This results in the death of Rosencrantz and Guildenstern. But the death of Polonius also brings about Laertes' enmity for Hamlet (especially since Polonius' death, together with Hamlet's behavior, seems responsible for Ophelia's madness and death). This enmity results in Laertes' agreeing to the fencing match. Yet the death of Polonius is accidental; i.e., Hamlet did not mean to kill him.

Is Hamlet too intellectual to act decisively?

It is sometimes said that intellectual activity incapacitates a man for action. Is this true of Hamlet? But why should thinking disable a man from acting? Montaigne, for instance, who was interested in the practical (i.e., moral) education of children, thought that philosophy was a very necessary part of their education for their future life of action.

If thinking about, say, courage and temperance is a hindrance to being courageous and temperate, would it not mean that all virtue consists simply in non-thinking, instinctual action? Or is our life of such a nature that the thinking man perceives genuine dilemmas while the non-thinking man rushes in "where angels fear to tread"? Which of them leads the happier life?

The following questions are designed to help you test the thoroughness of your reading. Each question is to be answered by giving a page or pages of the reading assignment. Answers will be found on page 190 of this Reading Plan.

1 In what connection does Hamlet say, "There is nothing either good or bad, but thinking makes it so"?

2 Why is Hamlet so amazed that an actor can rouse himself to such passion over Hecuba?

3 Hamlet compares his own inertia not only with the passion of actors, but also with that of another group of men. Who are they?

4 To what other beings does Hamlet compare man?

5 Who says, "Good night, sweet prince; / And flights of angels sing thee to thy rest!"?

6 What does Hamlet tell Ophelia he wishes for her if she marries?

7 What is Polonius' advice to his departing son, Laertes?

8 Concerning whom is Hamlet told, "Leave her to heaven"?

LOCKE

Concerning Civil Government (Second Essay)

Vol. 35, pp. 25–81

In the history of human liberty, Locke's essay *Concerning Civil Government* stands out not only as a great contribution to political theory, but also as an effective instigator of political action. It is a stirring pronouncement of the principles of the English "bloodless revolution" of 1688, which brought about fundamental innovations in the British constitution. It also set the stage for the American Revolution of 1776 by furnishing inspiration to the writers of the Declaration of Independence.

Its central doctrines of man's natural and unalienable rights, of popular sovereignty, and of the right of rebellion are eloquently set forth in the opening paragraphs of the Declaration. That all men are endowed "with certain unalienable rights," that "governments derive their just powers from the consent of the governed," and that when government becomes destructive of human rights, "it is the right of the people to alter or to abolish it"—these are the principles (and, for the most part, the words) which Thomas Jefferson and his associates adopted from Locke and put to good use.

While the image of good government that Locke had in mind was a constitutional monarchy, in which the legislative power of Parliament was supreme but in which the king retained certain executive prerogatives, the republican form of government set up by the Constitution of the United States is a more thoroughgoing embodiment of his ideal of government by law rather than by men. All our political liberties are rooted in the rule of law. It is this which makes constitutional government "free government"—government that secures to all of us "the blessings of liberty." No American can ever afford to forget this basic truth. The reading of Locke's essay will never permit him to.

Eleventh Reading

I

Locke's two essays on government were first published in 1690, the same year in which his *Essay Concerning Human Understanding* appeared. The date is of some significance, for it is just a year after the accession of William and Mary to the throne of England.

He wrote his political treatises in Holland, where he had gone into exile in 1683, returning to England six years later on the same ship which carried Princess Mary, the wife of William of Orange. In the preface to the two treatises, Locke expresses the hope that these works would

> establish the throne of our great restorer, our present King William —to make good his title in the consent of the people, which, being only one of all lawful governments, he has more fully and clearly than any prince in Christendom; and to justify to the world the people of England whose love of their just and natural rights, with their resolution to preserve them, saved the nation when it was on the very brink of slavery and ruin.

The first *Treatise on Civil Government* is directed against Sir Robert Filmer's *Patriarcha*, which upheld the theory that monarchs rule by divine right—a right supposedly transmitted from Adam. In the first chapter of the second treatise, Locke summarizes what he has shown in the first, and indicates what the subject matter of the second treatise is. If kings do not govern by divine right, and if government is more than the rule of the strongest (which hardly seems to deserve being dignified by the name "government"), then we must discover some other source for the authority of government. Accordingly, the full title of the second treatise is: *An Essay Concerning the True Original Extent and End of Civil Government.*

In other words, Locke did not believe that royal authority

was divinely given and therefore unchallengeable. Such a theory, of course, would have given the English throne to James II rather than to William of Orange. But if royal authority *is* challengeable, if a king may, upon cause, be deposed, who has the authority to say that a king should be dismissed and a new one installed? Who shall be the judge between a king and his people? In Chapter XIX of the second treatise (entitled "Of the Dissolution of Government") Locke answers the question:

> Who shall be judge whether the prince or legislative act contrary to their trust? . . . To this I reply, The people shall be judge . . . (p. 81b)

This treatise, therefore, is dedicated to establishing that the authority of governments derives from those whom they govern—a proposition which it succeeded in establishing so well that less than a hundred years later we read in the American Declaration of Independence:

> We hold these truths to be self-evident. . . . That, to secure these [natural] rights, governments are instituted among men, deriving their just powers from the consent of the governed . . . (Vol. 43, p. 1a)

II

Locke begins his quest for the legitimacy of government by defining political power:

> Political power, then, I take to be a right of making laws, with penalties of death, and consequently all less penalties for the regulating and preserving of property, and of employing the force of the community in the execution of such laws, and in the defence of the commonwealth from foreign injury, and all this only for the public good. (p. 25c–d)

Such power and the government which wields it comes into being, Locke maintains, as the result of a compact made by persons who previously lived in a non-political condition.

Locke is by no means the first political philosopher to have a "social contract" theory. For instance, the English philosopher Thomas Hobbes (1588–1679) had a fully developed theory of this sort. But there are great differences, nevertheless, between Hobbes's and Locke's view of the origin of the state.

These differences have to do with the condition of men prior to the formation of the state, and with the consequences that derive from living in a state. If men enter into civil society by making a contract among themselves, then they must first exist in a condition prior to the state. Both Hobbes and Locke call this the "state of nature"—that is to say, a condition which is natural to man. Here we may recall, by way of contrast, Aristotle's view that the political state is natural to man.

According to Hobbes, the state of nature is a state of war; men are either actually fighting each other or threatening each other. In such a state, Hobbes says, there are "no arts; no letters; no society; and which is worst of all, continual fear, and danger of violent death; and the life of man, solitary, poor, nasty, brutish, and short." (*Leviathan*, Vol. 23, Ch. 13, p. 85c)

But Locke does not view the state of nature (or, presumably, human nature itself) so darkly. Rather, he says, in the state of nature men enjoy "a state of perfect freedom to order their actions, and dispose of their possessions and persons as they think fit, within the bounds of the law of Nature, without asking leave or depending upon the will of any other man." (p. 25d)

Thus, while Hobbes thinks of the state of nature as one of war and brutishness, Locke thinks of it as a state of liberty. For there may be liberty either in the state of nature or in the state of civil society:

> The natural liberty of man is to be free from any superior power on earth, and not to be under the will or legislative authority of man, but to have only the law of Nature for his rule. The liberty of man in society is to be under no other legislative power but that established by consent in the commonwealth, nor under the dominion of any will, or restraint of any law, but what that legislative shall enact according to the trust put in it. Freedom, then, is not what Sir Robert Filmer tells us: "A liberty for every one to do what he lists, to live as he pleases, and not to be tied by any laws";

but freedom of men under government is to have a standing rule to live by, common to every one of that society, and made by the legislative power erected in it. A liberty to follow my own will in all things where that rule prescribes not, not to be subject to the inconstant, uncertain, unknown, arbitrary will of another man, as freedom of nature is to be under no other restraint but the law of Nature. (p. 29d)

Thus even the state of nature has a law, according to Locke:

The state of Nature has a law of Nature to govern it, which obliges every one, and reason, which is that law, teaches all mankind who will but consult it, that being all equal and independent, no one ought to harm another in his life, health, liberty or possessions . . . (p. 26b)

Locke himself makes his difference from Hobbes quite explicit in the following passage which we may assume has Hobbes in mind:

Here we have the plain difference between the state of Nature and the state of war, which however some men have confounded, are as far distant as a state of peace, goodwill, mutual assistance, and preservation; and a state of enmity, malice, violence and mutual destruction are one from another. (p. 29b)

From this difference their conceptions of the state of nature follows a difference in their views of the social contract and civil society. For Hobbes, man is in such a miserable state naturally that he gives up all rights upon entering civil society, in order only to be safe and protected from the lusts and passions of other men.

For Locke, too, man has something to gain from entering into the social contract. He enumerates the disadvantages of the state of nature as (1) lack of established and promulgated law, (2) absence of a judge to make determinations according to this law, and (3) lack of power to execute what is in accord with the law. But Locke hastens to add that men do not give up all their rights upon entering civil society:

But though men when they enter into society give up the equality, liberty, and executive power they had in the state of Nature into the hands of the society, to be so far disposed of by the legislative as the good of the society shall require, yet it being only with an intention in every one the better to preserve himself, his liberty and property (for no rational creature can be supposed to change his condition with an intention to be worse), the power of the society or legislative constituted by them can never be supposed to extend farther than the common good, but is obliged to secure every one's property by providing against those three defects above mentioned that made the state of Nature so unsafe and uneasy. (p. 54d)

And so describes the actual formation of political society as follows:

Men being, as has been said, by nature all free, equal, and independent, no one can be put out of this estate and subjected to the political power of another without his own consent, which is done by agreeing with other men, to join and unite into a community for their comfortable, safe, and peaceable living, one amongst another, in a secure enjoyment of their properties, and a greater security against any that are not of it. (p. 46d)

III

What Locke has to say about the origin of civil society is also of interest in connection with the concept of property. It is apparent that property is very important in Locke's political theory. He says that the law of nature commands one not to harm another's possessions; and he also says that men enter into society in order to preserve more perfectly their liberty and property. Thus the right to property is protected both by the law of nature and the civil law; in fact, one of the reasons for the existence of civil society is the preservation of property.

In Chapter V, Locke takes up the question of property in detail. By property Locke means private property; for that is a man's property which is his own. In this chapter, Locke considers how it comes about that anyone has private property, i.e., owns something to the exclusion of all others. He concludes that it is labor which gives the laborer a right to, or property in, that which he produces or adds his labor to. He summarizes his view as follows:

> Though the things of Nature are given in common, man (by being master of himself, and proprietor of his own person, and the actions or labour of it) had still in himself the great foundation of property . . .
>
> Thus labour, in the beginning, gave a right of property, wherever any one was pleased to employ it, upon what was common . . . (p. 34c)

We must realize that Locke uses the term "property" to refer not only to land or goods, but also to anything else that is a man's own, as the following passage indicates:

> Man being born, as has been proved, with a title to perfect freedom and an uncontrolled enjoyment of all the rights and privileges of the law of Nature, equally with any other man, or number of men in the world, hath by nature a power not only to preserve his property—that is, his life, liberty, and estate, against the injuries and attempts of other men, but to judge of and punish the breaches of that law . . . (p. 44a)

Since man has a natural right to property in this wider sense (i.e., life, liberty, and estate), the state cannot take it away from him, but must rather protect his right to it. The Declaration of Independence echoes Locke, substituting, however, "pursuit of happiness" for "estate":

> We hold these truths to be self-evident, that all men are created equal; that they are endowed by their Creator with certain unalienable rights; that among these are life, liberty, and the pursuit of happiness. That to secure these rights, governments are instituted among men . . . (Vol. 43, p. 1a)

IV

Aristotle said that the political state is natural. Locke says that the natural condition of man is that in which he existed prior to the origin of the state. What is the reason for this difference?

Such a difference of opinion can result from a different understanding of (1) what man is, or (2) what it means for something to be natural.

We can illustrate how differences in these concepts would

lead to differences concerning the naturalness of the state. It is completely natural for bees to form a kind of society, as every beehive illustrates. But there are many animals that live solitarily, i.e. not even in packs or herds; nevertheless they may occasionally be found in a group because of special circumstances. As an example of this consider tigers. They ordinarily live and hunt alone, yet they may live in a group in a zoo or menagerie. Such a group is clearly an artificial one.

Whether the state is natural or artificial depends, therefore, on whether human gregariousness is like that of bees, or is something imposed on men by artificial convention. This matter is further complicated, however. For the beehive comes about as the result of completely instinctual action, whereas those who maintain that the state is natural also agree that its origin is not due to instinct but to reason. Thus Aristotle distinguishes between the gregariousness of bees and that of men. Only the latter are *political* animals, because of their possession of speech and reason (see Vol. 9, p. 446b–c).

It is easier to see how differences in the meaning of "natural" affect the question. If "natural" means that which is normal, what occurs always or for the most part, then the political state is natural. If, on the other hand, "natural" means "original" or refers to any condition that is stripped of all complications, additions, and embellishments, or if it is taken to be the same as "primitive," then a pre-societal or pre-political condition may well be natural.

Does a "social contract" theory require us to believe that there actually was a time when men lived in a state of nature?

It is not always easy to see, in a given author, whether he treats the social contract as a fiction or a hypothesis—as something that must be imagined to have taken place in order to legitimize present governments—or whether he actually thinks there was such a historical event. Locke discusses the question on page 28b–c; we shall return to his answer below.

To give some examples of these opposing views, it seems on the whole safe to say that Rousseau thinks of the state of nature as a hypothesis; see for example the *Discourse on the Origin of Inequality*, Volume 38, pages 333c–334a. Kant appears to take a similar view in *The Science of Right*, Volume 42, page 437c–d. On the other hand, Hobbes says that although there was perhaps never a time when everyone in the world was in a state of nature, there are nevertheless even now many men in such a condition. (See *Leviathan*, Vol. 23, pp. 85d–86a.)

Are sovereign nations in a state of nature?

It seems in Locke's view that they are. And if they are, then this also has a bearing on the previous question. For even if man's living in a state of nature and entering a social contract turn out to be fictions, a state of nature among *nations* seems real enough, and so does the need for a social contract among them.

That sovereign nations are in a state of nature can be seen readily. No laws govern them; no nation is secure from the predatory attacks of another; the strongest nation enforces its will. Indeed it seems as though it is Hobbes's rather than Locke's conception of the state of nature that applies to nations.

Locke himself writes as follows:

> It is often asked as a mighty objection, where are, or ever were, there any men in such a state of Nature? To which it may suffice as an answer at present, that since all princes and rulers of "independent" governments all through the world are in a state of Nature, it is plain the world never was, nor never will be, without numbers of men in that state. (p. 28b)

A social contract among nations would, by analogy, require each nation to give up its "equality, liberty and executive power" in order to be more secure, in a society of nations, in its "life, liberty, and estates." In other words, a society of nations would require each nation to give up its sovereignty. Thus we see that the United Nations is not a political society, for each nation in it maintains its sovereignty, as is evidenced by the right of the veto in the Security Council and the immunity of the member states from the UN's "interference" in their internal affairs.

Since, according to social contract theories, a state is formed by the consent of all those who were in a state of nature, must the government of a civil society also be based on consent, i.e., must it be constitutional?

The answer is no, or at least uncertain. For Hobbes, although an adherent of the social contract theory of the origin of the state, is also a firm believer in the absolute power of governments once established; while Locke, as we have seen, is an advocate of constitutionalism, i.e., government based on the consent of the governed.

Curiously enough, however, both Hobbes and Locke derive their differing views as to the nature of government from their social contract theories. The difference is explained by their differing views of the state of nature.

For Hobbes, the state of nature is so terrible (nasty, brutish, and short) that men give up everything in order to get away from it. Thus they give up, forever, any rights against the sovereign. Locke, however, conceiving men to have liberties and rights in the state of nature, holds that no man would want to make his condition worse than it was, and therefore maintains that men always retain rights against the sovereign. Their consent, in other words, is conditional upon his executing the trust placed in him.

What, if anything, is the significance of substituting "life, liberty, and the pursuit of happiness" for "life, liberty, and estates" in the enumeration of natural rights?

Were the writers of the Declaration of Independence any less believers in the right to "estates" (i.e., private property) than Locke? That is hardly likely, if we examine the other writings of the Declaration's authors and signers.

Nor is it likely that the substitution is altogether insignificant, constituting merely a slip of the pen, or the substitution of a more euphonious phrase for one less so. There *was* disagreement among the Founding Fathers about the political significance of private property. Franklin, for example, opposing the limitation of suffrage to property-holders, asked, "Why should property be represented at all?"

"Pursuit of happiness" seems to take in a wider territory than "estate." Perhaps it can be maintained that that was the reason for the change. If pursuit of happiness requires a man's estate to be secure, then the Declaration of Independence affirms that to be part of man's inalienable right; but if other things are also required, it also asserts his right to those.

The following questions are designed to help you test the thoroughness of your reading. Each question is to be answered by giving a page or pages of the reading assignment. Answers will be found on page 191 of this Reading Plan.

1 What constitutes a man's *tacit* consent to the constitutional laws of a government?

2 Can the legislature delegate the power of making laws to any one else?

3 Who, in the state of nature, has the right to judge that the law of nature has been transgressed and to execute the punishment?

4 Which is the supreme power among the powers of government?

5 What is prerogative?

6 What are the limits to wealth-getting?

7 Is there a right of rebellion against government?

8 What is the distinction between usurpation and tyranny?

9 How can one man have despotical power over another?

SWIFT

Gulliver's Travels

Vol. 36, pp. xv–184

W e have seen that a number of the works already covered in this general introduction to the *Great Books* both prompt and help the reader to engage in self-examination. According to Socrates' counsel that "the unexamined life is not worth living," these books contribute to the worth of the individual life by increasing personal self-knowledge.

The injunction to "Know thyself" may be a counsel of wisdom for the human race as a whole as well as for the individual man. Just as the individual can become more alive through becoming more reflective, so mankind as a whole can profit from self-awareness. To the extent that satire has a kindly and constructive purpose, it aims to help mankind to achieve this by providing it with a portrait of itself that may not be in all respects either kindly or complimentary.

In the whole tradition of Western literature, *Gulliver's Travels* performs the satirical function more thoroughly than any other book. Swift's imaginative powers show us how the human race might appear to other creatures, smaller or larger, better or worse, than ourselves. Seeing ourselves as others see us cannot help being painful, even humiliating, but if we can conquer our impulse to dismiss as a vicious caricature Swift's picture of the human race, we as members of it may be helped by it to see our kind in truer perspective.

Twelfth Reading

I

One of the wonders of English literature is that *Gulliver's Travels* is so widely considered a children's book. It is, in fact, frequently sold in a children's edition, usually containing only the first two parts; and there are some people who are unaware of the existence of the Laputans and the Houyhnhnms.

The prevalent view is strange because there are few books which are more adult in their meaning or more devoid of the qualities of simple entertainment that are usually associated with children's literature. If one were to search for adjectives to describe Gulliver, they would have to come from a list of such as the following: satirical, biting, bitter, savage, merciless, mocking, contemptuous, misanthropic.

Swift does not like men or mankind. While his criticism is directed especially against his contemporary Englishmen, it is equally applicable to the human race as a whole. The devices which Swift uses to make his points (really just one point) are varied and, as we shall see, thoroughly cover the ground.

It is easy to see how the first two voyages, to Lilliput and to Brobdingnag, might give rise to some pleasant entertainment. The notion of an ordinary man finding himself first a giant, and then a midget, is amusing. All sorts of situations can be constructed that will make us laugh. Swift does not fail to imagine such situations; for instance, the picture of Gulliver drawing behind him an entire fleet of warships, full of little sailors and soldiers, is certainly enjoyable, and enjoyable to children. So are situations where Gulliver is on the opposite side of the scale: the notion of a man having to fight an ordi-

nary bird with a heavy cudgel, or being carried in the mouth
of a dog, is picturesquely ridiculous.

But Swift never stops with merely presenting pictures that
are funny because of the disproportion they display. He draws
the disproportion out to extremes, until it is no longer funny
and another and deeper meaning appears in it. In general it
may be said that the device which he uses is that of pushing
any human characteristic to its extreme, and thereby showing
what is wrong or even despicable in it.

In the first two parts, we may note that what he pushes to
extremes is not merely physical largeness and smallness. In an
extended sense, he shows us what happens when people become too large (i.e., gross or proud) or too small (i.e., petty or
mean).

His mercilessness can be instantly seen in the fact that
Gulliver seems worse than his surroundings, whether he is the
giant or the midget. One might think that if, relative to the
Lilliputians, he was too proud and inconsiderate, then at least
in comparison to the Brobdingnagians he would seem delicate,
gentle, and sensitive. Instead, however, we find that in these
first two parts of the book, no one comes off unscathed. Gulliver suffers by comparison with some of the Lilliputians and
some of the Brobdingnagians; these peoples, on the other hand,
are also used by the artist to depict extremes of foolish or con-
temptible human behavior.

II

The third part of the book is the least unified of the four, containing several voyages. It, too, is in no sense complimentary to
mankind, but it contains some observations that, while stinging
in their rebuke, are also highly amusing and shrewd com-
mentaries, especially on learning and scholarship.

Thus, Swift comments on the absent-mindedness of the
learned:

> It seems, the minds of these people are so taken up with intense
> speculations, that they neither can speak, or attend to the discourses

of others, without being rouzed by some external taction upon the
organs of speech and hearing; for which reason, those persons who
are able to afford it, always keep a flapper . . . in their family, as
one of their domesticks; nor ever walk abroad, or make visits, without him. And the business of this officer is, when two or more persons are in company, gently to strike with his bladder the mouth of
him who is to speak, and the right ear of him, or them, to whom
the speaker addresseth himself. (pp. 94b–95a)

And no reader will be able to forget the academy at Lagado,
where such projects flourish as that of

a most ingenious architect, who had contrived a new method for
building houses, by beginning at the roof, and working downwards
to the foundation. (pp. 107b–108a)

Then there is the proposal to abolish words and communicate
instead by means of things themselves:

Many of the most learned and wise adhere to the new scheme of
expressing themselves by *things*; which hath only this inconvenience
attending it; that if a man's business be very great, and of various
kinds, he must be obliged in proportion to carry a greater bundle
of *things* upon his back, unless he can afford one or two strong
servants to attend him. I have often beheld two of those sages almost sinking under the weight of their packs, like pedlars among
us; who, when they met in the streets would lay down their loads,
open their sacks, and hold conversation for an hour together; then
put up their implements, help each other to resume their burthens,
and take their leave. (p. 111b)

As always, however, Swift reserves his sharpest barbs for politics and politicians. He reports, for example, the following
scheme for reconciling opposing political factions:

You take an hundred leaders of each party; you dispose them into
couples of such whose heads are nearest of a size; then let two
nice operators saw off the occiput of each couple at the same time,
in such a manner, that the brain may be equally divided. Let the
occiputs thus cut off be interchanged, applying each to the head
of his opposite partyman. It seems indeed to be a work that re-
quireth some exactness; but the professor assured us, that if it
were dextrously performed, the cure would be infallible. For, he
argued thus; that the two half brains being left to debate the
matter between themselves within the space of one scull, would

soon come to a good understanding, and produce that moderation as well as regularity of thinking, so much to be wished for in the heads of those, who imagine they came into the world only to watch and govern its motion: and as to the difference of brains in quantity or quality, among those who are directors in faction; the doctor assured us from his own knowledge, that it was a perfect trifle. (p. 113b)

III

But it is in the land of the superhuman horses, the Houyhnhnms, that Swift rises to the peak of his satirical power, although at the same time he also comes closest to passing from satire to hatred.

The idea of endowing animals with human powers of speech and reason is not new, of course. Horses have been depicted before Swift as the superiors of men. In the *Iliad*, Homer tells us that Achilles' chariot was drawn by immortal horses. And after Achilles gives his armor and horses to his closest friend, Patroclus, and Patroclus is killed, the horses guard his body and weep. (See *Iliad*, Book XVII; Vol. 4, pp. 126b–127a.)

Swift's special invention, however, consists in showing us the other side of the coin. Not only does he make the Houyhnhnms the possessors of all that is best in man, but he also adds the Yahoos, giving them simultaneously human form and the most brutish characteristics. Here is how Swift describes the Yahoos:

> By what I could discover, the Yahoos appear to be the most unteachable of all animals, their capacities never reaching higher than to draw or carry burthens. Yet I am of opinion, this defect ariseth chiefly from a perverse, restive disposition. For they are cunning, malicious, treacherous and revengeful. They are strong and hardy, but of a cowardly spirit, and by consequence insolent, abject, and cruel. It is observed, that the *red-haired* of both sexes are more libidinous and mischievous than the rest, whom yet they much exceed in strength and activity. (p. 164b)

Compare this with what he says just a page later about the Houyhnhnms:

As these noble Houyhnhnms are endowed by nature with a general disposition to all virtues, and have no conceptions or ideas of what is evil in a rational creature, so their grand maxim is, to cultivate *reason,* and to be wholly governed by it. Neither is *reason* among them a point problematical as with us, where men can argue with plausibility on both sides of the question; but strikes you with immediate conviction; as it must needs do where it is not mingled, obscured, or discoloured by passion and interest. (p. 165a–b)

Since the whole book is written in the first person, we may imagine that what Captain Gulliver says, when he is forced to leave the land of Houyhnhnms and is picked up by a Portuguese ship, applies equally well to Swift:

In gratitude to the captain I sometimes sat with him at his earnest request, and strove to conceal my antipathy against human kind, although it often broke out, which he suffered to pass without observation. (p. 178b)

Surely only a man who truly despised mankind could write the following lines:

My wife and family received me with great surprize and joy, because they concluded me certainly dead; but I must freely confess, the sight of them filled me only with hatred, disgust and contempt. (p. 179b)

These words are taken from the next to the last chapter. Here and in the last chapter Swift almost entirely abandons any pretense of satire (which always conceals love or care) and turns instead to straight invective against humanity at large.

I V

What are the similarities and differences between satire and tragedy?

The question may seem a little farfetched. But there is this similarity: both tragedy and satire emphasize the insignificance of man. More important than this similarity is their difference. In tragedy, man is shown to be noble, or ennobled by his sufferings, even though those sufferings are due to his insignificance as opposed to the forces of fate and fortune. In satire, on the other hand, man's smallness is used not to stir noble emotions in the reader or spectator, but, rather, amused contempt.

Thus we can see that satire also shares certain characteristics with comedy; for both make fun of man's foibles and follies. But again the difference outweighs the sameness: whereas comedy emphasizes the humanity of man, satire paints man as less than human and as approaching the brute, or—as in the case of the Yahoos—as actually brutal.

Compare the following statements about man:

a "What is man, that thou art mindful of him? and the son of man, that thou visitest him?

"For thou has made him a little lower than the angels, and hast crowned him with glory and honour.

"Thou madest him to have dominion over the works of thy hands; thou hast put all things under his feet:

"All sheep and oxen, yea, and the beasts of the field;

"The fowl of the air, and the fish of the sea, and whatsoever passeth through the paths of the seas." (Psalms, 8:4-8)

b "Wonders are many, and none is more wonderful than man . . . speech, and wind-swift thought, and all the moods that mould a state, hath he taught himself. . . . Cunning beyond fancy's dream in the fertile skill which brings him, now to evil, now to good. . . ." (Sophocles, *Antigone*, Vol. 5, p. 134a–b)

c "For man, when perfected, is the best of animals, but, when separated from law and justice, he is the worst of all. . . . Wherefore, if he have not virtue, he is the most unholy and the most savage of animals, and the most full of lust and gluttony." (Aristotle, *Politics*, Book I, Chap. 2; Vol. 9, p. 446d)

d "What a piece of work is a man! how noble in reason! how infinite in faculty! in form and moving how express and admirable! in action how like an angel! in apprehension how like a god! the beauty of the world! the paragon of animals!" (Shakespeare, *Hamlet,* Act. II; Vol. 27, p. 43d) "He looked upon [men] as a sort of animals to whose share, by what accident he could not conjecture, some small pittance of *reason* had fallen, whereof we made no other use than by its assistance to aggravate our *natural* corruptions, and to acquire new ones which nature had not given us." (*Gulliver's Travels,* Pt. IV, Chap. VII; Vol. 36, pp. 159–160)

Which of the four parts of Gulliver's Travels *is most successful?*

The answer to this question will probably vary somewhat from person to person according to taste. But there are, nevertheless, some general observations that we can make.

In some respects the "Voyage to the Country of the Houyhnhnms" is clearly the most successful. It makes Swift's point most forcefully; it has the greatest shock value. Furthermore, in all the other parts, Captain Gulliver always finds something to criticize even in the countries to which he travels. The satire, therefore, is twofold. On the one hand, Swift shows up his contemporaries as fools by comparing their characteristics to the virtues of these foreigners. On the other hand, he exaggerates in these foreigners certain of the qualities of his countrymen to such an extent that their absurdity and even villainy become clear.

But in the "Voyage to the Country of the Houyhnhnms" all the virtue is on the side of the Houyhnhnms, and all the vice on the side of the Yahoos. This surely strengthens the force of the example. However, Swift also runs the danger here of being *too* savage.

We must ask ourselves, therefore, whether the weapon of satire does not lose some of its effectiveness when it is employed so ferociously by Swift. In addition, the whole of *Gulliver's Travels,* not just the "Voyage to the Country of the Houyhnhnms," raises the most disturbing questions as to the fixed and extreme views that one people, in real life, may form of another whom they do not know or with whom they may be at war.

The following questions are designed to help you test the thoroughness of your reading. Each question is to be answered by giving a page or pages of the reading assignment. Answers will be found on page 191 of this Reading Plan.

1   After his return to England from the land of the Houyhnhnms, what was the first thing that Captain Gulliver purchased in order to make his stay tolerable?

2   How do the immortals (Struldbruggs) live in Luggnagg?

3   What was the manner of approaching the king of Luggnagg?

4   Why did the king of Brobdingnag turn down Gulliver's offer to provide him with gunpowder?

5   What was the cause of the quarrel between the political parties in Lilliput? What was the cause of the quarrel between Lilliput and Blefuscu?

6   How are children educated in Lilliput?

7   What is the reward for law-abidingness in Lilliput?

8   What sentence was passed on Gulliver in Lilliput?

Thirteenth Reading

GIBBON

The Decline and Fall of the Roman Empire

Chaps. XV–XVI

Vol. 40, pp. 179–234

In the history of the West, there is no more momentous occurrence than the spread of Christianity. It is this event which gives social and political meaning to the division of history into B.C. and A.D. Though there are many threads of continuity in thought and culture which mark the common pattern of Western civilization, both pagan and Christian, the replacement of paganism by Christendom represents a profound—perhaps, the most profound—change in the moral and spiritual character of Western life. It revolutionized society and human life. It created new institutions and reformed old ones. It supplanted the Roman Empire as the tie which bound all the diverse peoples of the West together.

The conversion of the West to Christianity defies easy explanations. There is something mysterious about the process by which the faith of a handful of men in one generation became the religion of millions upon millions over the centuries. In these two chapters of *The Decline and Fall of the Roman Empire,* Gibbon acknowledges the mystery while at the same time undertaking to examine what happened with critical detachment in the light of historical evidence.

Whether or not we accept Gibbon's views on the natural and supernatural causes at work, whether or not we share or reject his skepticism, we are left in a state of wonder that is appropriate to the extraordinary character of the events described.

Thirteenth Reading

I

We must begin by noting again that it is unfair procedure to read, out of a very long book, only two chapters—chapters, furthermore, that come in the middle of the book. It is a procedure that is unfair to Gibbon, the Roman Empire, the Christian religion, and the reader.

But *The Decline and Fall of the Roman Empire* is an immensely long book, and these two chapters form a kind of whole, united as they are by their subject matter, Christianity. As long, then, as the reader is always aware that he cannot judge either Gibbon or the subject matter competently on the basis of a relatively short selection, he can safely and profitably permit himself to go ahead. Let us look briefly at the earlier chapters in order to see why Gibbon chose to insert these two chapters on Christianity at this point in his history.

Chapters XV and XVI deal with the early church up to the year A.D. 350. Thus they roughly cover the time before St. Augustine. Gibbon turns to the subject of Christianity at the chronological point in his history when he has reached the emperor Constantine the Great (who died in A.D. 337). With Constantine, Christianity became the official religion of the Roman Empire; and whereas, before then, empire and church had been two distinct and often opposed entities, after Constantine the history of the Roman Empire and the history of the Roman church are almost indistinguishably intertwined.

This is not to say that there were no more difficulties for Christianity. Even persecutions began again, most notably under the emperor Julian, surnamed the Apostate, who died in A.D. 363. But with the death of Julian, Christianity definitely and irrevocably became victorious. From then on its struggles were largely internal.

The 350 years which it took for the church to become triumphant are also the first 350 years of the Roman Empire. Gibbon briefly reviews the first two hundred years, beginning his detailed account with the time following the so-called golden age of the empire (after the death of Emperor Marcus Aurelius Antoninus, the Stoic philosopher, whose *Meditations* are included in Volume 12).

It may be useful to recall the names of the emperors during these two hundred years. Christ was born during the reign of Augustus, the adopted son of Julius Caesar; and the Julio-Claudian line of emperors continued as follows: Tiberius, Gaius (Caligula), Claudius, Nero. With the death of Nero, the Julio-Claudian emperors came to an end, and civil war ensued. There were, in the space of two years, three emperors in rapid succession, viz., Galba, Otho, and Vitellius. The armies then raised Vespasian to the throne, starting the Flavian line. This happened in A.D. 69. In the year 70, Vespasian's son Titus burned the city of Jerusalem. Titus later became emperor himself, and was followed by his brother, Domitian.

Incidentally, the vicissitudes of the empire from the time of Tiberius to that of Vespasian are recorded by Tacitus in the *Annals* and in the *Histories*, in Volume 15 of the Great Books. Gibbon himself quotes the famous passage in Tacitus dealing with the persecutions of the Christians under Nero. (See pp. 212b–213a)

After the assassination of Domitian, there follow the five "adoptive" emperors (so called because each adopted as his son the man he designated as his successor) during whose reigns the empire enjoyed perhaps its most prosperous and tranquil times. These emperors were, in order, Nerva, Trajan, Hadrian, Antoninus Pius, and Marcus Aurelius. Nerva acceded to the imperial office in A.D. 96; Marcus Aurelius died in 180. The first few sentences of Gibbon's work give his view of this period:

In the second century of the Christian era, the Empire of Rome comprehended the fairest part of the earth, and the most civilised portion of mankind. The frontiers of that extensive monarchy were guarded by ancient renown and disciplined valour. The gentle but powerful influence of laws and manners had gradually cemented the union of the provinces. Their peaceful inhabitants enjoyed and abused the advantages of wealth and luxury. The image of a free constitution was preserved with decent reverence: the Roman senate appeared to possess the sovereign authority, and devolved on the emperors all the executive powers of government. During a happy period (A.D. 98–180) of more than fourscore years, the public administration was conducted by the virtue and abilities of Nerva, Trajan, Hadrian, and the two Antonines.

The first map appended to Volume 40 will serve to confirm Gibbon's view. It shows the extent of the Roman Empire at the death of Trajan—and it clearly was immense.

From the death of Marcus Aurelius (180) to the accession of Constantine as undisputed emperor (323) there were more than twenty-five emperors. These turbulent times are treated by Gibbon in Chapters IV through XIV. When his history reaches Constantine, he is ready to take up the subject of Christianity.

II

Two things are probably most characteristic of these two chapters of *The Decline and Fall of the Roman Empire*. The first is Gibbon's attitude toward Christianity; the second, his style. The former of these is, of course, most clearly displayed here, since these chapters explicitly deal with Christianity; but Gibbon's style remains remarkable throughout the history.

The first sentence of Chapter XV gives us a clue to his conception of his task:

> A candid but rational inquiry into the progress and establishment of Christianity may be considered as a very essential part of the history of the Roman empire. (p. 179a)

"Candor" and "rationality" are the mottoes of Gibbon's inquiry; and often he seems to consider the two equivalent. "The theologian," he continues a few lines later,

> may indulge the pleasing task of describing Religion as she descended from Heaven, arrayed in her native purity. A more melancholy duty is imposed on the historian. He must discover the inevitable mixture of error and corruption which she contracted in a long residence upon earth, among a weak and degenerate race of beings. (p. 179b)

The weapons of Gibbon's wit are not always used on the orthodox church alone. Thus, speaking of the sect of Gnostics, he refers to their "many sublime but obscure tenets" (p. 184a), while a few pages later it is the Neo-Platonists who feel his sting with their "specious and noble principles" (p. 186b). Still, his sharpest barbs seem reserved for the Christians, as when he calls the Christian clergy "a celebrated order of men which has furnished the most important, though not always the most edifying, subjects for modern history" (p. 197a–b), or when, commenting on the fact that many early Christians lived in voluntary poverty, he remarks that their children often "found themselves beggars because their parents had been saints." (p. 197d)

Comments such as these may be taken as instances of Gibbon's candor; his rationality, however, is exemplified in the following passage:

> The names of Seneca, of the elder and the younger Pliny, of Tacitus, of Plutarch, of Galen, of the slave Epictetus, and of the emperor Marcus Antoninus, adorn the age in which they flourished, and exalt the dignity of human nature. They filled with glory their respective stations, either in active or contemplative life; their excellent understandings were improved by study; philosophy had purified their minds from the prejudices of the popular superstition; and their days were spent in the pursuit of truth and the practice of virtue. Yet all these sages (it is no less an object of surprise than of concern) overlooked or rejected the perfection of the Christian system. (p. 205d)

Gibbon, of course, lived in the age of enlightenment. It is natural that he should raise the question why these sages of antiquity, as enlightened as men could be, refused to take up the Christian religion. Nor is this all, for he goes on:

But how shall we excuse the supine inattention of the Pagan and philosophic world to those evidences which were presented by the hand of Omnipotence, not to their reason, but to their senses? During the age of Christ, of his apostles, and of their first disciples, the doctrine which they preached was confirmed by innumerable prodigies. The lame walked, the blind saw, the sick were healed, the dead were raised, daemons were expelled, and the laws of Nature were frequently suspended for the benefit of the church. But the sages of Greece and Rome turned aside from the awful spectacle, and pursuing the ordinary occupations of life and study, appeared unconscious of any alterations in the moral or physical government of the world. (p. 206b–c)

We can hardly avoid thinking that in Gibbon's opinion the unreasonableness and inattention was by no means all on the side of the ancient sages and philosophers.

III

We need not say much about Gibbon's style. The quotations we have already given also illustrate his mastery of the phrase. Most characteristic, perhaps, is the way in which he balances word against word, or phrase against phrase; often he uses words or phrases with opposed meanings to make the contrast sharper. Examples are "candid but rational inquiry," "sublime but obscure tenets," an order of men that "has furnished the most important, though not always the most edifying, subjects for modern history," etc.

The last sentence of the work offers a fine example of Gibbon's style, as well as being of interest for its content:

It was among the ruins of the Capitol that I first conceived the idea of a work which has amused and exercised near twenty years of my life, and which, however inadequate to my own wishes, I finally deliver to the curiosity and candour of the public. (Vol. 41, p. 598c)

IV

Is Gibbon's work invalidated because of his attitudes and opinions?

We certainly cannot maintain that it is completely invalidated. Indeed the article on Rome in *Encyclopædia Britannica* refers to Gibbon's work as one "which has never been superseded as a history of the entire imperial period."

At the same time, it clearly is also true that many of Gibbon's judgments cannot be taken at face value. It is, however, not very likely that a reader will be misled, for Gibbon's prejudices are not hidden.

This problem of the impartiality of a historian is a vexing one; we have encountered it before, in Plutarch and in Augustine. Neither of these two authors writes with complete impartiality or even pretends to. Plutarch is interested in biographical material that will illustrate his thesis (that the ancients excelled in the moral virtues of courage, temperance, and wisdom), while Augustine is interested in such autobiographical material as illustrates his thesis (that God is good and the cause of Augustine's conversion). Neither of these authors, however, considers himself technically a historian nor sets out, as Gibbon does, to write a general history.

How does the rise of Christianity relate to the decline and fall of the Roman Empire?

We may wonder whether Christianity contributed to the decline of the empire, or whether, on the other hand, it retarded that decline without being able to prevent it. That it had some influence on the course of the empire is very likely. The establishment of a new religion as the official religion of the civilized world could not help having its effects also on the political and social side.

No doubt some of the effects, especially in the early days of Christianity, were disruptive of the general peace and harmony of the empire. Persecutions of a portion of the population brought on by a sense that this portion isolated itself from the rest of the empire cannot be good; nor can the spectacle of some emperors embracing, and others repudiating, this new religion.

On the other hand, some effects must clearly have been of benefit to the empire. Christianity had a unifying effect, and long after Rome had lost its military and political strength (being replaced in this respect by Constantinople), the peoples of the West looked toward Rome as the spiritual center of their world.

Is Gibbon a determinist in history?

The meaning of the question is this: does Gibbon seem to think that history moves in a pattern that is unchangeable, according to laws of its own, so that it accomplishes its end necessarily? Such a view leaves no room for free will and maintains instead that human freedom is an illusion, since each individual merely plays a predetermined part.

This is an extreme statement of the deterministic position; but Gibbon would appear to be at least a partial adherent to it. He maintains, for instance, that the growing luxury and degeneracy of Rome in the second century A.D. made her eventual fall inevitable, though perhaps the details of her destruction might not yet be determined. It is the doctrine of historical inevitability, in other words, that makes a historian a determinist.

In looking for an answer to this question, it must of course be remembered that any historian is looking for the causes of the historical events that he describes. Such a search for causes does not make the historian a determinist; only if each cause is the necessary and inevitable consequent of its antecedent causes do we have a doctrine of determinism.

What were the strengths and weaknesses of the Christian religion?

The difficulty with this question is to sort out from Gibbon's account what were the *real* strengths and weaknesses. We must try to find a middle course between one extreme view which finds the history of the early church riddled with foolishnesses and abuses and the opposite extreme which simply ascribes all successes of the church to divine intervention. Neither explanation is easy to sustain on historical grounds. The former view ignores the fact that Christianity *did* succeed, while the latter offers no explanation of that fact on the level of human history.

In other words, since Christianity and the church are here treated as part of human history, we must find human explanations for their vicissitudes.

The following questions are designed to help you test the thoroughness of your reading. Each question is to be answered by giving a page or pages of the reading assignment. Answers will be found on page 191 of this Reading Plan.

1 What were the rules that Trajan laid down for the prosecution of persons suspected of being Christians?

2 How many Christians suffered martyrdom in the persecutions of Diocletian and his successors?

3 How many Christians were there in Antioch during the reign of Theodosius?

4 What are the three ways of escaping persecution that a Christian might take?

5 How was the struggle between Paul of Samosata and the orthodox church settled?

6 Does Gibbon believe in the miracles of the early church? When does he think miracles ceased to take place?

The Declaration of Independence

Vol. 43, pp. 1–3

The Constitution of the United States

Vol. 43, pp. 11–20

The Federalist

Vol. 43, Nos. 1–10, pp. 29–53; No. 15, pp. 62–66;

No. 31, pp. 103–105; No. 47, pp. 153–156;

No. 51, pp. 162–165; Nos. 68–72, pp. 205–218

It would be natural to assume that the schooling of every American included the reading of the Declaration of Independence, the Constitution of the United States, and *The Federalist*. If there is any relation at all between schooling and preparation for intelligent citizenship, this much firsthand acquaintance with the principles and institutions of our government should be given to all of our country's future citizens in the course of their schooling. But very few of the graduates of our colleges, and even fewer of those who have completed high school, have ever seen the inside of *The Federalist*, and many have never even heard the work mentioned. The number—at either level of schooling—who have carefully read the Declaration and the Constitution is almost as small.

The adult who reads *The Federalist* for the first time will enjoy the sense of acquiring an understanding of his government which should be the property of every citizen. More than that, he will be struck by the clarity and power of both the thought and the writing. They exemplify the common level of political discourse in the days when this republic was founded. The articles which comprise *The Federalist* were current political journalism in the years 1787-1789. They were written for newspaper readers. If we contemplate that fact, and compare the level of their style and substance with that of political speeches, articles, or journalism in our own day, we are compelled to wonder about the education of our political leaders as well as of our citizens today.

Fourteenth Reading

I

The Declaration of Independence is largely the work of Thomas Jefferson, while Alexander Hamilton is the chief author of *The Federalist*, although some papers were contributed by James Madison and some by John Jay. In spite of the fact that the contribution of the latter two is quantitatively small, their co-authorship was important, since Madison was one of the chief framers of the Constitution, while John Jay's prestige, at the time of writing, was the greatest of the three men. He was the oldest of the three authors (forty-two); Hamilton was only thirty years old, and Madison, thirty-six. No matter who the author of a Federalist paper is, it is always signed "Publius."

The Constitution was, of course, the collaborative effort of the Constitutional Convention, but Madison is often called the "Father of the Constitution."

The Constitutional Convention completed its work in September 1787, and the Federalist papers started to appear soon thereafter. They were articles written for several New York newspapers, in order to urge the people of the state of New York to ratify the Constitution. The papers appeared from October 1787 to April 1788. There was considerable opposition to ratification in New York, led by the very influential governor, George Clinton.

The last article of the Constitution provides that if nine of the thirteen states ratify it, it shall then go into effect among those nine states. In spite of the efforts of the Federalist papers, New York was among the last states to ratify the Constitution; and in fact it did not ratify until after the ninth state

(New Hampshire) had done so. (With New Hampshire's ratification, the Constitution went into effect for the ratifying states.) Even when New York finally ratified in July 1788, it did so only by a very slight margin of votes in its convention—thirty to twenty-seven.

II

Jefferson's views on representative government were in many respects opposed to the views of the Federalist writers. Jefferson favored placing power and responsibility in the hands of the people as far as possible; the Federalists wanted safeguards against the uses to which the people might put such power. Jefferson, for example, wrote as follows to Pierre Du Pont de Nemours:

> We both consider the people as our children, and love them with parental affection. But you love them as infants whom you are afraid to trust without nurses; and I as adults whom I freely leave to self-government.

Madison, on the other hand, thinks that it is beneficial to take the management of government out of the direct hands of the people and to delegate it to elected representatives, because this will

> refine and enlarge the public views, by passing them through the medium of a chosen body of citizens, whose wisdom may best discern the true interest of their country, and whose patriotism and love of justice will be least likely to sacrifice it to temporary or partial considerations. (p. 52a)

Thus, he prefers representative, republican government to direct democracy, not only because the size and population of the United States make the latter impracticable, but because he (unlike Jefferson) thinks that the people cannot always be trusted to know what is for their own good. "Under such [republican] regulation," he continues,

> it may well happen that the public voice, pronounced by the representatives of the people, will be more consonant to the public good than if pronounced by the people themselves. . . . (p. 52a)

The Constitution contains many evidences of these two opposed tendencies, one of which would give power and responsibility to the people, while the other would guard against unlimited popular government. The success of the Constitution may, at least in part, be attributed to the fact that it managed successful compromises between these two tendencies.

Let us look at some of these compromises. They can be found everywhere. Thus in Article 1, it is noted that the Congress of the United States "shall consist of a Senate and House of Representatives." The bicameral arrangement of the legislature constitutes a compromise between a Congress that is very responsive to the will of the people, and a Congress that acts in the light of its own best opinion, without necessarily and automatically succumbing to popular pressure.

One reason why the House of Representatives is very responsive to the wishes of the electorate is that each one of its seats is up for election every two years. In the Senate, however, only a third of the seats *can* change at each election; so that not only does each senator serve for six years, but the over-all complexion of the Senate tends to change more slowly than that of the House. Furthermore, as Section 3 of this article points out, the senators were not to be elected by the people, but chosen by the legislature of each state. This procedure was not changed until the seventeenth amendment, which provided that senators as well as representatives were to be elected by the people of each state, became effective in 1913.

The manner of electing the president also reveals the opposing tendencies in the Constitution. On the one hand, the president is elected by the people, rather than by the state legislatures or governors. This places great power in the hands of the people. On the other hand, the election of the president is not direct; the people of each state elect electors, who in turn elect the president. This interposition of the electoral college which, in theory, is free to name as president whomever it likes, was intended to limit the power of the people;

the college has, as we know, become a mere formality.

Yet another instance of this conflict can be seen in the duties of each branch of the legislature. Only the popular house can initiate bills having to do with money matters (presumably because taxation is to go along with representation), but only the upper house is consulted in matters of foreign policy (presumably because it is not subject to sudden and disastrous whims). Or, again, only the House of Representatives has the power to initiate impeachment; but the Senate tries all cases of impeachment.

III

In *The Federalist*, No. 10, Madison faces one of the perennial problems that beset any popular government—the problem of internal instability, strife, and faction. It is a problem well known to modern democracies. An extreme contemporary instance is the rapid succession of governments in France. Examples such as this always raise a doubt as to whether the people are really fit to govern themselves. But let us hear Madison's description of the problem:

> Complaints are everywhere heard from our most considerate and virtuous citizens, equally the friends of public and private faith, and of public and personal liberty, that our governments are too unstable, that the public good is disregarded in the conflicts of rival parties, and that measures are too often decided, not according to the rules of justice and the rights of the minor party, but by the superior force of an interested and overbearing majority. (p. 49d)

Such malfunctioning of government, Madison says, is largely due to factions, i.e., groups of citizens which manage to control the government not for the common good, but for their own special interests. To prevent this development, he says, we can either (1) eliminate the causes of factions, or (2) control their effects.

Factions can be eliminated if it is possible to give to every citizen "the same opinions, the same passions, and the same interests." But this clearly is impossible. The other method of eliminating a faction is that of "destroying the liberty which is essential to its existence." But, Madison adds,

> It could never be more truly said than of [this] remedy, that it was worse than the disease. Liberty is to faction what air is to fire, an aliment without which it instantly expires. But it could not be less folly to abolish liberty, which is essential to political life, because it nourishes faction, than it would be to wish the annihilation of air, which is essential to animal life, because it imparts to fire its destructive agency. (p. 50b)

Hence Madison concludes that the way to deal with factions is to realize that they will always be with us and to concentrate on controlling their effects. Now a factious group, i.e., a group aiming at its own rather than the common good, becomes dangerous when it becomes the majority in a popular government. Only then can it pursue its selfish ends without effective opposition. Therefore, the remedy which Madison proposes is something which will prevent a faction from becoming the ruling power in a government.

> It may be concluded that a pure democracy, by which I mean a society consisting of a small number of citizens, who assemble and administer the government in person, can admit of no cure for the mischiefs of faction. A common passion or interest will, in almost every case, be felt by a majority of the whole; a communication and concert result from the form of government itself; and there is nothing to check the inducements to sacrifice the weaker party or an obnoxious individual. Hence it is that such democracies have ever been spectacles of turbulence and contention. . . . (p. 51c–d).

The solution which Madison advocates is republican rather than democratic government. "The two great points of difference between a democracy and a republic are," he points out,

> first, the delegation of the government, in the latter, to a small number of citizens elected by the rest; secondly, the greater number of citizens, and greater sphere of country, over which the latter may be extended. (pp. 51d–52a)

We have already quoted Madison's opinion that such delegates will often recognize the true interest of the country (as distinguished from the selfish interest of a faction) better than the people themselves could. Furthermore, a larger country suffers less from the evils of factions than a small one, for the following reasons:

> Extend the sphere, and you take in a greater variety of parties and interests; you make it less probable that a majority of the whole will have a common motive to invade the rights of other citizens; or if such a common motive exists, it will be more difficult for all who feel it to discover their own strength, and to act in unison with each other. (p. 52c–d)

So convinced is Madison that the Constitution will prevent the evils of factions that he concludes the tenth paper thus:

> In the extent and proper structure of the Union, therefore, we behold a republican remedy for the diseases most incident to republican government. (p. 53a)

IV

The separation of the powers of government is a basic provision of the Constitution of the United States. It is a device that prevents any part of the government from becoming too powerful.

Locke mentions the separation of powers; but the doctrine that it is all-important for free government stems from Montesquieu, as Madison acknowledges in *The Federalist*, No. 47. After first distinguishing the three powers, Montesquieu says:

> When the legislative and executive powers are united in the same person, or in the same body of magistrates, there can be no liberty; because apprehensions may arise, lest the same monarch or senate should enact tyrannical laws, to execute them in a tyrannical manner.
>
> Again, there is no liberty, if the judiciary power be not separated from the legislative and executive. Were it joined with the legislative, the life and liberty of the subject would be exposed to arbitrary control; for the judge would be then the legislator. Were it joined to the executive power, the judge might behave with violence and oppression.
>
> There would be an end of everything, were the same man or the same body, whether of the nobles or of the people, to exercise

those three powers, that of enacting laws, that of executing the public resolutions, and of trying the causes of individuals. (*The Spirit of Laws*, Book XI, Chap. 6; Vol. 38, pp. 70a–b)

In *The Federalist*, No. 47, Madison notes the importance of the separation of powers:

> One of the principal objections inculcated by the more respectable adversaries to the Constitution is its supposed violation of the political maxim, that the legislative, executive, and judiciary departments ought to be separate and distinct. In the structure of the federal government, no regard, it is said, seems to have been paid to this essential precaution in favour of liberty. The several departments of power are distributed and blended in such a manner as at once to destroy all symmetry and beauty of form, and to expose some of the essential parts of the edifice to the danger of being crushed by the disproportionate weight of other parts. (p. 153a)

Madison acknowledges that there is considerable mixing of governmental powers (the so-called system of checks and balances) in the proposed Constitution. But, referring to Montesquieu's words and to his primary example (the British Constitution), Madison argues that Montesquieu

> did not mean that these departments ought to have no *partial agency* in, or no *control* over, the acts of each other. His meaning, as his own words import, and still more conclusively as illustrated by the example in his eye, can amount to no more than this, that where the *whole* power of one department is exercised by the same hands which possess the *whole* power of another department, the fundamental principles of a free constitution are subverted. (p. 154b–c)

Still, even if we grant that some mixture of powers is defensible, they are for the most part to be kept separate. And so the author of *The Federalist*, No. 51, continues as follows:

> To what expedient, then, shall we finally resort, for maintaining in practice the necessary partition of power among the several departments, as laid down in the Constitution? The only answer that can be given is, that as all these exterior provisions are found to be inadequate, the defect must be supplied, by so contriving the interior structure of the government as that its several constituent

parts may, by their mutual relations, be the means of keeping each other in their proper places. (p. 162d)

"Publius" then lists the principal means for achieving this end:

> In order to lay a due foundation for that separate and distinct exercise of the different powers of government, which to a certain extent is admitted on all hands to be essential to the preservation of liberty, it is evident that each department should have a will of its own; and consequently should be so constituted that the members of each should have as little agency as possible in the appointment of the members of the others. . . .
>
> It is equally evident, that the members of each department should be as little dependent as possible on those of the others, for the emoluments annexed to their offices. . . .
>
> But the great security against a gradual concentration of the several powers in the same department, consists in giving to those who administer each department the necessary constitutional means and personal motives to resist encroachments of the others. The provision for defence must in this, as in all other cases, be made commensurate to the danger of attack. Ambition must be made to counteract ambition. The interest of the man must be connected with the constitutional rights of the place. (pp. 162d–163b)

In a word, the Federalists propose to rely on the self-interest of men. If the self-interest of men can be made to coincide with the separation of governmental powers, then these powers will be kept separate far more surely than by any artificial or external devices. "Publius" dwells for a moment on the melancholy truth that public interest is safest when it coincides with private ambition:

> It may be a reflection on human nature that such devices should be necessary to control the abuses of government. But what is government itself but the greatest of all reflections on human nature? If men were angels, no government would be necessary. If angels were to govern men, neither external nor internal controls on government would be necessary. In framing a government which is to be administered by men over men, the great difficulty lies in this: you must first enable the government to control the governed; and in the next place oblige it to control itself. (p. 163b–c)

V

What, according to the Federalists, is the indispensable condition of civil peace?

Papers 2 through 9 are devoted to the discussion of war and peace. The first four of these deal with the "dangers from foreign force and influence" while the last four are concerned with "dangers from war between the states."

In *The Federalist*, No. 6, Hamilton makes it clear that if the states were to become independent, sovereign nations, they would soon become embroiled in war.

> A man must be far gone in Utopian speculations who can seriously doubt that, if these States should either be wholly disunited, or only united in partial confederacies, the subdivisions into which they might be thrown would have frequent and violent contests with each other. To presume a want of motives for such contests as an argument against their existence, would be to forget that men are ambitious, vindictive, and rapacious. (p. 39a)

He takes up this topic again a little later:

> There are still to be found visionary or designing men, who stand ready to advocate the paradox of perpetual peace between the States, though dismembered and alienated from each other. The genius of republics (say they) is pacific; the spirit of commerce has a tendency to soften the manners of men, and to extinguish those inflammable humours which have so often kindled into wars. (p. 40a)

Hamilton shows by many examples that this is a delusion. "There have been," he concludes, "almost as many popular as royal wars." The only effective means of maintaining peace among the several States is by uniting them under a common government. Hamilton quotes the Abbé de Mably in support of his contention: "Neighbouring nations are naturally enemies of each other, unless their common weakness forces them to league in a confederate republic, and their constitution prevents the differences that neighbourhood occasions, extinguishing that secret jealousy which disposes all states to aggrandise themselves at the expense of their neighbours." (p. 41c)

Are there any first principles or axioms in politics?
In *The Federalist*, No. 31, Hamilton writes as follows:

> In disquisitions of every kind, there are certain primary truths, or first principles, upon which all subsequent reasonings must depend. These contain an internal evidence which, antecedent to all reflection or combination, commands the assent of the mind. . . . Of this nature are the maxims in geometry, that "the whole is greater than its part; things equal to the same are equal to one another; two straight lines cannot enclose a space; and all right angles are equal to each other." Of the same nature are these other maxims in ethics and politics, that there cannot be an effect without a cause; that the means ought to be proportioned to the end; that every power ought to be commensurate with its object; that there ought to be no limitation of a power destined to effect a purpose which is itself incapable of limitation. (p. 103c)

Obviously, therefore, Hamilton answers our question affirmatively. But we can still ask whether he is correct, and even if he is, whether he has correctly identified the first principles of politics.

Taking the first question first, we may point out that some of the axioms to which Hamilton refers are not restricted to geometry. Indeed, such axioms, being "common notions," apply equally to geometry, arithmetic, ethics, or any other discipline. In other words, that the whole is greater than any of its parts is not a truth applicable only to geometry.

Hence, strictly speaking, there are no "axioms of geometry" or "axioms of politics," but simply "axioms." On the other hand, there are first or basic principles of geometry; and there may also be first or basic principles of politics.

That a straight line cannot enclose a space seems to be such a first principle of geometry. This principle is definitely geometrical in nature. Most of the statements concerning power that Hamilton offers appear to be first principles of politics, rather than axioms.

This brings us to a second question: Are the first principles of politics only those that Hamilton mentions? Or, for instance, is the observation that the public interest is most effectively safeguarded when it coincides with private interest also a first principle?

Are the self-evident truths of the Declaration of Independence first principles of politics?

In the second paragraph of the Declaration, we read:

> We hold these truths to be self-evident, that all men are created equal; that they are endowed by their Creator with certain unalienable rights; that among these are life, liberty, and the pursuit of happiness. That, to secure these rights, governments are instituted among men, deriving their just powers from the consent of the governed; that, whenever any form of government becomes destructive of these ends, it is the right of the people to alter or to abolish it, and to institute a new government, laying its foundation on such principles, and organizing its powers in such form, as to them shall seem most likely to effect their safety and happiness. (p. 1a)

It is interesting to observe that, although the Declaration of Independence preceded *The Federalist* by eleven years, Hamilton does not refer to the truths that Jefferson had called self-evident in order to exemplify the first principles of politics. The reason may be that Hamilton did not think these statements true, much less self-evident.

The twenty-second amendment to the Constitution limits the president to two terms. What are the consequences of this limitation?

Here is the precise text of the twenty-second amendment, which became effective on February 26, 1951:

> 1. No person shall be elected to the office of the President more than twice, and no person who has held the office of President, or acted as President, for more than two years of a term to which some other person was elected President shall be elected to the office of the President more than once. But this Article shall not apply to any person holding the office of President when this Article was proposed by the Congress, and shall not prevent any person who may be holding the office of President, or acting as President, during the term within which this Article becomes operative from

holding the office of President or acting as President during the remainder of such term.

2. This article shall be inoperative unless it shall have been ratified as an amendment to the Constitution by the legislatures of three-fourths of the several States within seven years from the date of its submission to the States by the Congress.

We may, first of all, wonder whether this amendment is an expression of one of the two tendencies in the Constitution that we mentioned earlier. Does this limitation of the president's tenure put greater or less power into the hands of the people? It probably does both. On the one hand, it prevents a president from becoming too powerful, because he continues in office too long. This, therefore, seems to safeguard the people against an ambitious president. On the other hand, the amendment also limits the power of the people, since it forbids them to elect anyone president for a third time, even if they should desire to do so because of his special qualifications or because of special circumstances.

Hamilton devotes all of paper No. 72 to exactly this question. He concludes that

> Nothing appears more plausible at first sight, nor more ill-founded upon close inspection, than a scheme which in relation to the present point has had some respectable advocates,—I mean that of continuing the chief magistrate in office for a certain time, and then excluding him from it, either for a limited period or for ever after. (p. 216d–217a)

He lists the various undesirable effects that he thinks would follow upon such a constitutional exclusion.

"One ill effect of the exclusion would be a diminution of the inducements to good behaviour." (p. 217a)

"Another ill effect of the exclusion would be the temptation to sordid views, to peculation, and, in some instances, to usurpation." (p. 217b)

"A third ill effect of the exclusion would be the depriving the community of the advantage of the experience gained by the chief magistrate in the exercise of his office." (p. 217d)

"A fourth ill effect of the exclusion would be the banishing men from stations in which, in certain emergencies of the state, their presence might be of the greatest moment to the public interest or safety." (p. 217d)

"A fifth ill effect of the exclusion would be, that it would operate as a constitutional interdiction of stability in the administration." (p. 218a)

Hamilton concludes his discussion with the following paragraph:

> There is an excess of refinement in the idea of disabling the people to continue in office men who had entitled themselves, in their opinion, to approbation and confidence; the advantages of which are at best speculative and equivocal, and are overbalanced by disadvantages far more certain and decisive. (p. 218d)

The following questions are designed to help you test the thoroughness of your reading. Each question is to be answered by giving a page or pages of the reading assignment. Answers will be found on page 191 of this Reading Plan.

1 What does the Constitution say about states' rights?

2 What do the writers of the Declaration of Independence lay down as the rights of free and independent states?

3 How, according to Hamilton, is the election of the president guarded against corruption?

4 What does Hamilton think is the main fault of the Articles of Confederation as compared with the Constitution?

5 What article and section of the Constitution made an amendment necessary for the collection of a graduated federal income tax?

6 What are the ingredients which make for a strong and vigorous president?

7 What does "Publius" consider to be the just causes of war?

MARX-ENGELS

Manifesto of the Communist Party

Vol. 50, pp. 415–434

"For a general about to fight an enemy," Gilbert K. Chesterton once said, "it is important to know the enemy's numbers, but still more important to know the enemy's philosophy." In the divided world in which we live, the Communist *Manifesto* furnishes us with a most compact and emphatic statement of the philosophy that governs or affects the other half of the world's population. In the struggle that is now going on between East and West, our obligation to examine this document with care is as great as the obligation to deepen our understanding of the Declaration of Independence. But to discharge this obligation is more difficult, for the Communist *Manifesto*, while deceptively easy to read, does not readily yield its central principles or its full implications.

When we grasp its principles and its implications, we may come to realize that reading the Communist *Manifesto* is almost as important for understanding the revolutionary changes that have taken place in our own society during the last thirty years, as it is for understanding the revolution which has changed the course of life for the teeming populations of Russia and China. While there can be no question in our minds that the political systems of West and East differ most radically with regard to the freedoms they protect or destroy, we may begin to question the character and extent of the differences between the economic systems of the East and the West.

We may be surprised to learn that capitalism as it exists in the United States and Great Britain today has been profoundly affected by the program set forth in the *Manifesto of the Communist Party,* and that our understanding of contemporary capitalism requires us to understand the socialism or communism which exists in Russia and China. When we realize this, we will also recognize that the spread of such understanding among us is of critical importance for the future of our political democracy and our free institutions.

Fifteenth Reading

I

The *Manifesto of the Communist Party* was written in 1847 and published the following year. Engels himself supplies us with important background information in the Preface:

> The *Manifesto* was published as the platform of the Communist League, a workingmen's association, first exclusively German, later on international, and, under the political conditions of the Continent before 1848, unavoidably a secret society. (p. 415a)

The specter of Communism, which the authors said was "haunting Europe" when they wrote the *Manifesto* in 1847, seemed to become a reality in 1848. A revolutionary movement swept through almost all the great nations of the Continent, the most notable exception being Russia. While in Great Britain it amounted to little more than a Chartist demonstration, violent insurrections took place in the capitals of the three great monarchies, Paris, Vienna, and Berlin.

At first, the revolutionaries were successful in wringing concessions from the governments; for instance, assemblies convened to draft constitutions for Prussia, Austria, and Germany. But these victories were temporary. The armies, which had remained faithful to their governments, soon repressed the insurgents. The concessions that had been made were for the most part withdrawn, although some advances toward constitutionalism and increased suffrage resulted in France, Prussia, and Austria.

Nevertheless, absolute monarchy was re-established in Germany, Austria, and Italy. In France, the reaction to the revolution led to the re-establishment of the hereditary empire in 1852, with Napoleon III as emperor. In this climate of reaction and suppression, there was no place for the authors of the *Manifesto*, and both eventually went to England where they spent the rest of their lives. It was there that Marx wrote his immense classic, *Capital*, the first volume of which was published in 1867.

The Preface to the English translation of the *Manifesto* in 1888 was written by Engels alone; Marx had died in 1883. But in this Preface, Engels refers to his and Marx's joint preface to the German edition of 1872. Twenty-five years had then passed since the writing of the *Manifesto*. The authors note that the "general principles laid down in this *Manifesto* are, on the whole, as correct as ever." (p. 417a) But they also note that historical conditions were already quite different in 1872 from what they were in 1847, and that, consequently, the practical recommendations of the *Manifesto* were already partly outdated.

II

Although the *Manifesto* is a short polemical work, it contains so many different yet important things that it is difficult to discern its structure. At least four different lines of thought seem to run through the *Manifesto*. We may call them (1) the *historical* strain, (2) the *prophetic* strain, (3) the *moral* strain, and (4) the *revolutionary* strain. One reason why it is difficult to read the *Manifesto* is that these four strains are not kept separate. On any given page, in any given paragraph, the authors are likely to be speaking with several of these purposes in mind.

1. *The Historical Strain.* A good bit of the early portion of the *Manifesto* is historical. Marx and Engels trace the development of the bourgeoisie "from the ruins of feudal society." The latter, they say, was doomed by such events as the discovery of America (which enormously increased the economic markets) and the Industrial Revolution (which enormously increased productive capacity). "We see, therefore," the authors conclude their rapid survey,

how the modern bourgeoisie is itself the product of a long course of development, of a series of revolutions in the modes of production and of exchange. (p. 420b)

Because of the tremendous changes which the bourgeoisie has brought about—changes of an economic and political sort, as well as changes in the structure of society—we read that "the bourgeoisie has played a most revolutionary role in history." (p. 420c)

The rapid and revolutionary changes brought about by the bourgeoisie win approval from Marx and Engels.

> The bourgeoisie, by the rapid improvement of all instruments of production, by the immensely facilitated means of communication, draws all nations, even the most barbarian, into civilization. . . .
> The bourgeoisie has subjected the country to the rule of the towns. It has created enormous cities, has greatly increased the urban population as compared with the rural, and has thus rescued a considerable part of the population from the idiocy of rural life. (p. 421c)

We shall see, in a moment, when we turn to the prophetic strain in the *Manifesto,* that this approval of the bourgeoisie extends only to its past role and to its overthrow of feudalism. But we must first consider some of the other historical subjects that the authors consider.

A subject that deeply concerns them is the terrible condition of the workers in the factories of the early nineteenth century. Their writing on this topic, although part of the historical strain, is primarily moral in character and intent. We shall, therefore, defer consideration of this matter until we come to deal with Marx and Engels as moralists.

In the Preface to the *Manifesto,* Engels states why he and Marx are so concerned with historical developments of classes and class struggles.

> In every historical epoch the prevailing mode of economic production and exchange, and the social organization necessarily following from it, form the basis upon which is built up, and from which alone can be explained, the political and intellectual history of that epoch; consequently, the whole history of mankind (since the dissolution of primitive tribal society, holding land and common

ownership) has been a history of class struggles, contests between exploiting and exploited, ruling and oppressed classes; the history of these class struggles forms a series of evolutions in which, nowadays, a stage has been reached where the exploited and oppressed class—the proletariat—cannot attain its emancipation from the sway of the exploiting and ruling class—the bourgeoisie—without at the same time, and once and for all, emancipating society at large from all exploitation, oppression, class distinctions and class struggles. (p. 416c–d)

The paragraph above states a philosophy of history. Its thesis is that the course of history has a definite pattern—one ruling class succeeding another in a series of evolutions—and that a definite point in history has now been reached where there will be just one more revolution, which will make the proletariat the ruling class.

2. *The Prophetic Strain.* The Marxist philosophy of history thus leads from purely historical to prophetic considerations. For this philosophy of history not only tells us how to interpret past events; it also predicts, on the basis of the pattern which it claims to see in history, what will happen next. More particularly, it predicts the proletarian revolution.

Not only will the proletarian revolution take place; it will also, in the Marxist view, necessarily be successful. For the bourgeoisie, which once played a revolutionary and progressive role in history, has now reached the point where it cannot long survive the onslaught of the proletariat. Bourgeois society carries within itself the seed of its own destruction.

Its destruction comes about through the economic crises which periodically result from overproduction. The bourgeoisie has no way of coping with them except by expanding its markets and further increasing production (see p. 422b-c). But as industry advances, the proletariat as a class increases; it finally realizes its own existence as a class and unites. "The development of modern industry," Marx and Engels write at the end of Chapter I,

cuts from under its feet the very foundation on which the bourgeoisie produces and appropriates products. What the bourgeoisie, therefore, produces above all are its own grave-diggers. Its fall and the victory of the proletariat are equally inevitable. (p. 425b)

But with the victory of the proletariat, the pattern of history will change. The proletarian revolution will "have swept away the conditions for the existence of class antagonisms and of classes generally, and will thereby have abolished its own supremacy as a class." (p. 429b) The pattern of history, in other words, is based on the class struggle. When classes disappear, so will the class struggle, and a utopian condition will prevail:

> In place of the old bourgeois society, with its classes and class antagonisms, we shall have an association in which the free development of each is the condition for the free development of all. (p. 429c)

3. *The Moral Strain.* We have already mentioned the authors' indignation about the exploitation of workers and their inhuman working conditions. Actually, they deal with this matter more explicitly in other works. Engels had already published *The Condition of the Working Class in England in 1844.* It describes in detail such things as the length of the working day (twelve, fourteen, or more hours), the unsanitary condition of both factories and worker's homes, and the almost unbelievable sacrifice of children to the factory system. Similarly, Marx in *Capital* treats of these abuses at considerable length. It is well to remember that both Marx's and Engel's sources are the official reports of factory inspectors and of royal investigating commissions—reports capable of arousing revolutionary fury in any morally sensitive person. In the *Manifesto,* addressed to the workers themselves, these conditions are referred to only cursorily; they are treated hurriedly, for instance, on pages 422c–423a.

A second moral consideration, very important in Marxist theory but also just touched on here, is the exploitation of the laborer. Marx and Engels denounce what they consider the basic bourgeois view of labor as a commodity. The wages of labor are just sufficient to enable workers to stay alive and reproduce. The benefits of labor all go to the bourgeoisie or capitalists. Labor and only labor, Marx and Engels say, is able to produce capital, yet the laborer receives none of it and the capitalist all of it.

> In bourgeois society living labour is but a means to increase accumulated labour. In Communist society accumulated labour is but a means to widen, to enrich, to promote the existence of the labourer. (p. 426b)

The "accumulated labour" which according to the authors is produced by "living labour" is, of course, capital.

4. *The Revolutionary Strain.* Marx and Engels propose two ways of attacking and overthowing capitalism. On the one hand, they propose a number of reforms that can be accomplished by law and, perhaps, without violence. On the other hand, they advocate a violent uprising of the workers.

These must not be understood as alternative means for bringing about the Communist revolution. They are supplementary to each other.

The reform program which Marx and Engels advocated in 1847 is set forth in the ten points listed on page 429a–b. We have already observed the fact that, in the Preface, Engels calls "this program . . . in some details antiquated." It is also interesting to note how many of these ten measures have now actually been instituted in bourgeois or capitalist countries.

The *second* proposal, a heavy progressive or graduated income tax, is in effect almost everywhere.

The *third* proposal, abolition of all right of inheritance, is partially realized through inheritance taxes which diminish the power of passing on wealth through inheritance.

The *fifth* proposal, calling for a national bank and centralization of credit in the hands of the state, has not been put into effect in the United States. There are, however, many countries with national banks. In the United States credit, though not exclusively in the hands of the state, is nevertheless controlled by governmental agencies like the Federal Reserve Bank.

The *sixth* proposal, centralization of the means of communication and transport in the hands of the state, has been followed in many countries. In every European country, for instance, the railways are nationalized.

The measures proposed in the *seventh* point are all in effect in the United States. The government operates some factories, either alone or in partnership with private business; it is in the irrigation and soil conservation business.

There are no industrial armies in this country, as proposed in the *eighth* point. But during the depression of the 1930's, we had something like such "armies"; for instance the CCC and the WPA.

The gradual abolition of the distinction between town and country, as envisaged in the *ninth* point, is going on right now.

The *tenth* proposal has been most fully realized in the United States. Free universal education is a fact, and the number of students attending institutions of higher learning is constantly on the increase. Abuses such as child labor are prevented by federal and state legislation.

The main proposal that has not been put into effect is the *first* one, which calls for the abolition of property in land. We shall return to this proposal about property in one of the questions to follow.

Finally, we should note what Marx and Engels have to say about the resort to violence to attain the ends of Communism:

> The Communists disdain to conceal their views and aims. They openly declare that their ends can be attained only by the forcible overthrow of all existing social conditions. Let the ruling classes tremble at a Communist revolution. The proletarians have nothing to lose but their chains. They have a world to win. (p. 434d)

III

What position do Marx and Engels take with regard to property?

"The theory of the Communists," they write, "may be summed up in the single sentence: abolition of private property." And subsequently they say that the Communist revolution they are proposing will be "the most radical rupture with traditional property-relations"; for in that revolution the proletariat will wrest "all capital from the bourgeoisie" and will centralize the ownership of "all instruments of production in the hands of the State."

These statements help us understand the question we are here considering. The kind of property that will change hands in the transition from the bourgeois to the Communist society is not the ownership of the things men consume from day to day—their food, their clothes, their personal belongings. It is the ownership of capital—the instruments of production. Such property will not be abolished, but the ownership of it will be radically transformed. All instruments of production will pass from private to public ownership. What will be abolished, in short, is *private* property in *capital* instruments.

Marx and Engels point out that the "abolition of existing property relations is not at all a distinctive feature of Communism. . . . The French Revolution, for example, abolished feudal property in favor of bourgeois property. The distinguishing feature of Communism," they continue, "is not the abolition of property generally, but the abolition of bourgeois property," that is, the private ownership of the instruments of industrial production. And in the very next sentence, they give what appears to be the reason for the abolition of bourgeois property; namely, that it is the "most complete expression of the system of producing and appropriating products that is based on class antagonisms, on the exploitation of the many by the few."

Under the bourgeois system of production, Marx and

Engels contend, wage labor creates capital, but not for the laborer. Under the Communist system of production, the capital that is created by human labor will be shared by the laborers. Through public ownership, capital will become the "common property" of all. The laborer will no longer be exploited, for the fruit of his labor will no longer be used *against* him, but *for* him, "to enrich, to promote the existence of the labourer."

The Communist plan to abolish private ownership of the means of production thus seems to be based on the proposition that private property in capital is the cause of the evils to be remedied—the exploitation of the working masses and the inhuman condition of their lives, to which Marx and Engels could so effectively point in the middle of the nineteenth century. The remedy prescribed seems to fit the cause. Since capital itself cannot be abolished, and since Marx and Engels see no sense in returning to pre-industrial methods of production, they advocate transferring the ownership and management of capital to the state under the dictatorship of the proletariat and for its benefit.

But there are other passages in the Communist *Manifesto* which point to another possible cause of the trouble, and hence suggest another remedy. Consider the following passage, in which Marx and Engels, addressing their remarks to the bourgeois capitalists of their day, say:

> You are horrified at our intending to do away with private property. But in your existing society private property is already done away with for nine-tenths of the population; its existence for the few is solely due to its non-existence in the hands of those nine-tenths. You reproach us, therefore, with intending to do away with a form of property, the necessary condition for whose existence is the non-existence of any property for the immense majority of society. (p. 426c–d)

In this passage, Marx and Engels seem to place the blame, not on the private ownership of capital, but rather on the fact that it is concentrated in the hands of the few. Such concentration necessarily makes the great mass of the population propertyless. It divides the population into the few who are the capitalists and the many who are the proletariat.

But if it is the *concentrated* ownership of capital rather than merely the *private* ownership of it which is the cause of the evils to be cured, then should not the remedy be the *diffused* private ownership of capital rather than the public, or state, ownership of it? In their day, Marx and Engels might not have thought it possible for the private ownership of capital to become ever more widely diffused, so that more and more men would become capitalists. What would they have said if they could have envisaged this possibility?

Would they then have recommended the abolition of all private capitalists, thereby making the state the only capitalist? Might they then have seen that making the state the only capitalist would result in the most concentrated form of ownership and management of the instruments of production, namely, by the bureaucrats who run the State?

The Communist Manifesto *predicted the collapse of capitalism as the result of the ever-widening gap between overproduction and underconsumption. Why has not this prediction come true?*

We can think about this matter by asking ourselves two questions. (1) What did *not* happen in the development of capitalism, which would have made the prediction come true? (2) What *did* happen, which the *Manifesto* did not anticipate?

The *Manifesto* itself gives us a clue to the answer. As Marx and Engels saw it in their day, "the average price of wage labour is the minimum wage, i.e., the quantum of the means of subsistence which is absolutely requisite to keep the labourer in bare existence as a labourer. What, therefore, the wage labourer appropriates by means of his labour merely suffices to prolong and reproduce a bare existence." Furthermore, they thought that keeping wages down to a bare subsistence level was the very essence of the capitalist system, and would always be the case.

If they had been right on this point, their prediction might have come true. With wages kept at a subsistence level, the working masses of the population would not have the purchasing power to buy more than a small portion of the consumable goods produced in ever-increasing quantities in an industrial economy. Although the small number of capitalists would have more than ample purchasing power, there is a natural limit to how much of the wealth produced they can consume. Hence with so much of the purchasing power concentrated in the hands of the few, the market would dry up and the capitalists would be faced with ever more serious business depressions until the cycle of boom-and-bust ended in the ultimate collapse of capitalism.

What Marx and Engels did not anticipate is that, in the course of the hundred years since 1848, the real wages of labor would steadily rise and that a widely diffused purchasing power would be created to sustain the market for the increasing quantities of consumable goods which capitalism is able to produce. The last serious economic depression in the United States occurred almost thirty years ago. Both labor leaders and capitalists in the United States think that we have found a way to avoid the kind of depression which occurred in the 1930's and which had been occurring regularly in the period between 1850 and 1930.

This leaves us with two questions to ponder. What are the specific changes we have introduced into our capitalist economy which have so far succeeded in preventing the collapse of capitalism that the Communist *Manifesto* predicted? And to what extent are the changes we have introduced in line with the ten specific measures proposed by Marx and Engels for the gradual overthrow of capitalism (listed on p. 429a–b)? Is capitalism thus being overthrown—or strengthened?

The following questions are designed to help you test the thoroughness of your reading. Each question is to be answered by giving a page or pages of the reading assignment. Answers will be found on page 191 of this Reading Plan.

1 What do Marx and Engels mean by the term "bourgeoisie"? What by the term "proletariat"?

2 Why is only the proletariat a really revolutionary class, among all the classes that are opposed to the bourgeoisie?

3 How do Marx and Engels view the bourgeois family?

4 Is Communism compatible with nationalism?

5 To which country did the Communists propose to pay most attention?

6 In the view of Marx and Engels, what determines people's ideas and conceptions?

ANSWERS

*to self-testing
questions*

First Reading

1. 200c–203c
2. 203c
3. 202d
4. 204c–205c
5. 206d, 211b–212a
6. 216d–219c

Second Reading

1. 296a–d
2. 310b–c
3. 311c–312b
4. 316c–318b
5. 319a–c
6. 320c–d
7. 321a–324c

Third Reading

1. 102b–103a
2. 104c–d
3. 108a–b
4. 108c–109a
5. 131a–132a; 135d–136b
6. 139a–140b
7. 141b–c

Fourth Reading

1. 339d–340a; 343d
2. 345b–c
3. 346b–c
4. 340a
5. 344a
6. 340d–341b
7. 347d–348c

Fifth Reading

1. 446c–d
2. 446d–447a
3. 449b
4. 451a
5. 452d
6. 453b–c
7. 454b–455c

Sixth Reading

1. 35a–b
2. 36a–b
3. 36d–38b
4. 46c–47a
5. 54a–55b
6. 59c–d
7. 543c–d
8. 546b–c
9. 564d–566a
10. 594a–595c
11. 599d–600a
12. 600c–601a

Seventh Reading

1. 1:6–12, 2:1–6
2. 2:9
3. 6:8–10
4. 14:7–12
5. 28:28
6. 42:6

Eighth Reading

1. 14c–d
2. 27c–d
3. 45d–47a
4. 60d–61a
5. 30c–31a
6. 39a–c
7. 9a
8. 36c–d

Ninth Reading

1. 118a–c
2. 59c–60a
3. 66b–c
4. 70d–71c
5. 77d–78c
6. 48c–49d

Tenth Reading

1. 43b
2. 46b–d
3. 59a–c
4. 43c–d
5. 71d
6. 48b–c
7. 35a–b
8. 37d

Eleventh Reading

1. 52c–53c
2. 58a–b
3. 26c–28b
4. 59d
5. 62b–d
6. 33a–c, 35a–36a
7. 75d–81d, esp. 80d–81b
8. 70d–71a
9. 65b–c

Twelfth Reading

1. 180a
2. 127a–129a
3. 122b–123b
4. 77a–78b
5. 21b–23a
6. 29b–31a
7. 28b
8. 35a–37a

Thirteenth Reading

1. 215c–216a
2. 233a–c
3. 202a–c
4. 220d–221b
5. 224b–d
6. 189d–190c

Fourteenth Reading

1. 18a
2. 3b
3. 205b–206a
4. 64b
5. 13d
6. 210c–211a
7. 33d

Fifteenth Reading

1. 419b
2. 424b–c
3. 427b–428a
4. 428a
5. 434b–d
6. 428b–d

ADDITIONAL READINGS

1. In connection with Plato, *Apology* and *Crito:*

The history of Socrates' life and death is continued in the *Phaedo* (Vol. 7, pp. 220–251). Socrates discusses, among other things, whether the soul is immortal. The *Meno* (Vol. 7, pp. 174–190) also affords glimpses of Socrates' personality, as well as a statement of his views on virtue and knowledge.

2. In connection with Plato, *The Republic:*

The discussion of justice and of the state is continued in *The Republic*, Books III–X (Vol. 7, pp. 324–441). Such famous things as Plato's views on education and the role of women in the state can be found in Books III–V (Vol. 7, pp. 324–373). Another discussion of justice, pitting Socrates against men even more irascible than Thrasymachus, is found in the *Gorgias* (Vol. 7, pp. 252–294).

3. In connection with Sophocles, *Oedipus the King* and *Antigone:*

Sophocles has a third tragedy centered around Oedipus and his family. This is *Oedipus at Colonus* (Vol. 5, pp. 114–130); its time of action is between that of the other two Theban plays. If you would like to read more Greek tragedy, you can try all or part of Aeschylus' trilogy (sometimes called the *Oresteia*), consisting of *Agamemnon* (pp. 52–69), *Choephoroe* (pp. 70–80), and *Eumenides* (pp. 81–91). These, however, should be read in that order. The third great Greek tragedian, Euripides, is also included in this volume. You may want to read his *Medea* (pp. 212–224). Or you might want to compare Euripides' *Electra* (pp. 327–339) with Sophocles' *Electra* (pp. 156–169).

4. In connection with Aristotle, *Nichomachean Ethics:*

After the first book of the *Ethics,* Aristotle turns to a discussion of the virtues. In Book V (Vol. 9, pp. 376–387) he discusses the virtue of justice. He returns to the subject of happiness in Book X (pp. 426–436).

5. In connection with Aristotle, *Politics:*

The various types of constitution, including democracy, are discussed by Aristotle in *Politics,* Books III–IV (Vol. 9, pp. 471–502).

6. In connection with Plutarch, *The Lives of the Noble Grecians and Romans:*

If you enjoyed reading Plutarch, there are many more *Lives* to choose from. For instance, here are two famous and brilliant traitors: "Alcibiades," "Coriolanus," and "Alcibiades and Coriolanus Compared" (Vol. 14, pp. 155–195). In "Demosthenes," "Cicero," and "Cicero and Demosthenes Compared" (pp. 691–725) Plutarch gives us two famous orators and statesmen.

7. In connection with the Book of Job:

Other "wisdom books" of the Bible are Proverbs, Psalms, and Ecclesiastes. The problem of divine justice and punishment is treated at length in Dante's *Divine Comedy,* especially *Hell* (Vol. 21, pp. 1–52). The notion of a wager between God and the devil is also employed in Goethe's *Faust* (Vol. 47); see the "Prologue in Heaven," pages 7–9.

8. In connection with St. Augustine, *The Confessions:*

The remainder of *The Confessions* (Books IX–XIII; Vol. 18, pp. 61–125) is less autobiographical. Augustine turns to the consideration of the difficult problems of memory, time, and the creation of the world. In *The City of God*, Book V (Vol. 18, pp. 207–230), Augustine discusses the doctrine of fate. He uses the Roman Empire as an example of divine government.

9. In connection with Montaigne, *The Essays:*

Here again there are a great many essays to choose from. You may wish to try "That Men Are Not to Judge of Our Happiness till after Death" (Vol. 25, pp. 26–28), or "That to Study Philosophy Is to Learn to Die" (pp. 28–36), or "Of Friendship" (pp. 82–88), or "Upon Some Verses of Virgil" (pp. 406–434).

10. In connection with Shakespeare, *Hamlet:*

All of Shakespeare's plays are contained in Volumes 26 and 27. To name some other tragedies: *King Lear* (Vol. 27, pp. 244–283), *Macbeth* (Vol. 27, pp. 284–310). Two historical plays that you will find fascinating are *Henry IV*, Parts I and II (Vol. 26, pp. 434–502).

11. In connection with Locke, *Concerning Civil Government:*

For a theory of the state of nature and the origin of government that is quite different from Locke's and Hobbes's theory, try Rousseau, *The Social Contract*, Books I and II (Vol. 38, pp. 387–406).

12. In connection with Swift, *Gulliver's Travels:*

If you would like to read more satire, less bitter than Swift's but just as learned, try Rabelais, *Gargantua and Pantagruel*, Books I and II (Vol. 24, pp. 1–126).

13. In connection with Gibbon, *The Decline and Fall of the Roman Empire:*

Another good unit in Gibbon, less specialized than the chapters you have read are Chapters 1–3 (Vol. 40, pp. 1–34). They cover the period of time just before the decline of the empire started in earnest. A good deal of the same time is covered by Tacitus, in the *Annals* (Vol. 15, pp. 1–184) and in the *Histories* (Vol. 15, pp. 189–302).

14. In connection with the American State Papers and *The Federalist:*

You might be interested in reading the Articles of Confederation (Vol. 43, pp. 5–9) as well as some other numbers of *The Federalist.* A theory of democracy is expounded by J. S. Mill in *Representative Government,* especially Chapters 1–8 (Vol. 43, pp. 327–389).

15. In connection with Marx and Engels, *Manifesto of the Communist Party:*

. More details of Marx's view of capitalism and how it produces surplus value through the exploitation of labor, can be found in *Capital,* Parts I–III (Vol. 50, pp. 13–151). You may want to compare what Adam Smith has to say on similar subjects in *The Wealth of Nations,* Book I (Vol. 39, pp. 1–116).